CW00418769

LEICESTER CITY
On This Day

LEICESTER CITY
On This Day

History, Facts & Figures
from Every Day of the Year

MATT BOZEAT

LEICESTER CITY
On This Day

History, Facts & Figures from Every Day of the Year

All statistics, facts and figures are correct as of 1st September 2008

© Matt Bozeat

Matt Bozeat has asserted his rights in accordance with the Copyright, Designs and Patents Act 1988 to be identified as the author of this work.

Published By:
Pitch Publishing (Brighton) Ltd
A2 Yeoman Gate
Yeoman Way
Durrington
BN13 3QZ

Email: info@pitchpublishing.co.uk
Web: www.pitchpublishing.co.uk

First published 2008

A catalogue record for this book is available from the British Library.

10-digit ISBN: 1-9054112-8-6
13-digit ISBN: 978-1-9054112-8-3

Printed and bound in Great Britain by Cromwell Press

To everyone who has helped me.
You know who you are.

Matt Bozeat – September 2008

FOREWORD BY ALAN BIRCHENALL

Unlike most of you reading this, I wasn't born a Leicester City fan. I was adopted by the club 37 years ago – and what a journey it has been since then.

I came to Leicester back in 1971 as a player because the club had a reputation for playing football the right way and having fantastic supporters. There have been lots of comings and goings since then, but that hasn't changed.

Great players have played for Leicester City. I was lucky enough to play alongside the likes of Keith Weller, Frank Worthington and Peter Shilton and we've seen legends such as Gary Lineker, Gary McAllister and Steve Walsh since then and too many other great players to mention.

I wouldn't claim to have been as good as any of them, but I would like to think City fans thought I was okay.

I used to give it 100 per cent every time I went on to the pitch – and I still do now for a club that has been good to me.

I've seen everything in my time at Leicester City; promotions, relegations, cup triumphs at Wembley and more false dawns than I care to remember.

I remember leaving Filbert Street after a thrashing of Sunderland believing that in Emile Heskey and Stan Collymore we had a forward partnership that could help establish Leicester as a real force in the Premier League.

A few days later, Heskey left!

I'm still here – and would love to be for many more years to come.

Alan Birchenall MBE – September 2008

INTRODUCTION

Back in the spring of 1884, a group of Old Wyggestonians met in a garden shed just off Fosse Road in Leicester and decided to form a football club.

Fast forward around 124 years and I'm sitting in a flat on Fosse Road, a short walk from where it all started, having just completed a book that hopefully charts all the major events that have touched our lives as Leicester City supporters since that first meeting.

Every promotion, relegation battle, classic game… they are all here and hopefully reading this book will bring back a lot of memories for you. Writing it brought back a lot of memories for me.

I would like to thank everyone at Pitch Publishing for their support and guidance. Thanks also to Leicester City historian Dave Smith for all his help and Alan Birchenall for writing the foreword. Also thanks to my family, friends and especially my dad for taking me to Filbert Street for the first time as a six-year-old.

Matt Bozeat – September 2008

LEICESTER CITY
On This Day

JANUARY

MONDAY 1ST JANUARY 1979

Gary Lineker made his Leicester City debut in a 2-0 win over Oldham Athletic at Filbert Street in a Division Two fixture. He didn't score, was dropped and had to wait more than three months for his first goal. Dave Buchanan grabbed the headlines against Oldham when he became City's youngest ever Football League debutant and youngest ever goalscorer at the age of 16 years 192 days.

SATURDAY 2ND JANUARY 1982

Jock Wallace's Leicester City started their FA Cup bid with a 3-1 win over Division One visitors Southampton at Filbert Street. A crowd of 20,598 saw Alan Young's powerful header send City on their way to victory. Young added another goal and Gary Lineker bagged the other for the Foxes with Kevin Keegan notching the Saints' reply.

FRIDAY 2ND JANUARY 1951

The television cameras came to Filbert Street for the first time to capture the action in an amateur international between England and Wales.

SATURDAY 3RD JANUARY 1987

Steve Moran bagged a hat-trick for Leicester City in a stunning 6-1 demolition of Sheffield Wednesday at Filbert Street. Alan Smith (2) and Paul Ramsey got the others.

SATURDAY 3RD JANUARY 1998

Leicester City took on Northampton Town in the third round of the FA Cup and there were those predicting an upset. Martin O'Neill's team were without a win in their previous five games and the Cobblers were going well in Division Two. But the visitors were never in the game. Ian Marshall, Garry Parker (penalty), Robbie Savage and Tony Cottee got the goals in a 4-0 romp and the visitors had defender Ian Clarkson sent off in the second half following a stamp on Muzzy Izzet.

SATURDAY 3RD JANUARY 2000

Matt Elliott's brace ensures Leicester City start the new Millennium with a 2-2 draw at Everton. The result ends a run of four successive defeats for the Foxes.

SATURDAY 4TH JANUARY 1992

Richard Smith volleyed in a last-gasp winner against top-flight visitors Crystal Palace at Filbert Street to send Leicester City into the draw for the fourth round of the FA Cup for the first time since 1985.

SATURDAY 5TH JANUARY 1985

Gary Lineker grabbed a hat-trick in the FA Cup third round clash with Burton Albion at Derby County's Baseball Ground, and then had it erased from the record books. The FA ordered the game to be replayed behind closed doors after Burton goalkeeper Paul Evans was struck by a missile thrown from the crowd. Alan Smith (2) and Steve Lynex also had goals wiped off after the FA's ruling.

SATURDAY 5TH JANUARY 1980

Neil Prosser popped up with an injury-time leveller for Isthmian League side Harlow Town at Filbert Street and Jock Wallace's Leicester City were heading for FA Cup humiliation. Martin Henderson had put Leicester ahead on 27 minutes and they should have had several more before the minnows secured a replay in the dying moments of the third round clash.

SATURDAY 5TH JANUARY 1991

David Pleat's Leicester City fell apart at Millwall in an FA Cup third round tie. They had both Paul Ramsey and Steve Walsh sent off and the lead given them by Tony James was wiped out by goals from the Lions in the 86th and 89th minutes.

SATURDAY 6TH JANUARY 1979

Keith Weller wore white tights while playing for Leicester City against Norwich City in the FA Cup third round at Filbert Street and scored a typically spectacular solo goal in a 3-0 win. He went on a run that took him past three challenges before firing home. It proved to be his last goal for the Foxes. Weller had earlier crossed for Larry May to put Leicester ahead. Martin Henderson bagged the third while Andy Peake also made his debut for the Foxes.

FRIDAY 7TH JANUARY 2000

Leicester City legend Ken Keyworth died in Rotherham, Yorkshire.

SUNDAY 8TH JANUARY 2006

Leicester City, struggling in the Championship under Craig Levein, took on Premier League Tottenham Hotspur at Filbert Street in the third round of the FA Cup. The game was going with the form book when the visitors took a 2-0 first-half lead in front of the BBC television cameras. Elvis Hammond gave Leicester hope, Stephen Hughes smashed in a second-half leveller and the Foxes snatched last-gasp glory when Mark De Vries made amends for an earlier miss by rolling home the winner in the dying seconds.

WEDNESDAY 8TH JANUARY 1992

Paul Fitzpatrick's diving header in the pouring rain in front of around 8,000 Leicester City fans at Meadow Lane sent Brian Little's team through to the northern final of the Zenith Data Systems Cup. His goal secured a 2-1 win for the Foxes after Tommy Wright had earlier cancelled out Craig Short's opener for the home side. The win set up a two-legged clash against Nottingham Forest with the winners going through to face the southern winners in the final at Wembley.

TUESDAY 8TH JANUARY 1980

Leicester City were beaten by non-league opposition in the FA Cup for the first time since 1914-15. John Mackenzie's goal secured a famous giant-killing for Harlow Town at their cramped Hammarskjold Road Sports Centre after a 1-1 draw.

SATURDAY 9TH JANUARY 1932

Ernie Hine bagged five goals as Leicester City romped to a 7-0 win at Crook Town in the FA Cup. Arthur Chandler and Walter Langford got the other goals for the Foxes.

SATURDAY 10TH JANUARY 1914

A cracking FA Cup fifth round tie against Tottenham Hotspur at Filbert Street saw Claude Stoodley's four goals haul Leicester City into a 5-3 lead with just ten minutes left. Spurs hit back to level and then won the replay 2-0.

WEDNESDAY 11TH JANUARY 1956

Arthur Rowley's hat-trick fired Leicester City to a 4-0 win at Luton Town in an FA Cup third round tie. Bill Gardiner got the other goal.

WEDNESDAY 11TH JANUARY 1978

Emile Heskey was born in Leicester.

SATURDAY 11TH JANUARY 1975

Mark Wallington started his spell of 331 consecutive games in goal for Leicester City in a 3-0 defeat at Everton in Division One.

WEDNESDAY 12TH JANUARY 2000

Leicester City went through to the quarter-finals of the League Cup after a thrilling clash against Fulham at Filbert Street. Geoff Horsfield, who went on to play for City, looked to have put the game beyond the home side when he netted after 75 minutes to make it 2-0 to the visitors. Steve Walsh's misdirected pass had led to Horsfield's goal and he set about making amends in stunning style with his rampaging run leading to Ian Marshall pulling a goal back. Walsh then sent the game into extra time with an equaliser. Fulham went ahead again, but Marshall made it 3-3 and Leicester held their nerve in the penalty shoot-out to go through 3-0.

SATURDAY 13TH JANUARY 1934

Leicester City started their bid for the FA Cup with a 3-0 win over Lincoln City at Filbert Street. The goals came from Arthur Maw, Arthur Lochhead and Jim Paterson.

SUNDAY 13TH JANUARY 1990

David Pleat's side self destructed on Tyneside. They led 4-2 at Newcastle United with just 16 minutes left and lost a nine-goal thriller with future Foxes boss Mark McGhee the last-gasp goal hero. David Oldfield made his Leicester City debut after joining in an exchange deal that took Wayne Clarke to Manchester City and the sides were level at 2-2 at the break. Tommy Wright and Steve Walsh were on target and Gary McAllister and Kevin Campbell put Leicester in charge at 4-2 before it all went wrong.

SATURDAY 14TH JANUARY 1984

Gary Lineker hit a hat-trick in a 5-2 win at Notts County in Division One. Kevin MacDonald and Andy Peake got the others.

SATURDAY 14TH JANUARY 1950

Willie Frame played his 459th and last game for Leicester City in the 3-0 defeat at Blackburn Rovers.

THURSDAY 16TH JANUARY 1997

Matt Elliott decided to join Leicester City, rather than Southampton, from Oxford United in a £1.6m deal.

SATURDAY 17TH JANUARY 2004

Micky Adams' Leicester City were stunned as Middlesbrough netted twice in injury time to snatch a point from their Premiership clash at the Riverside Stadium. Juninho put the home side ahead, latching on to a poor clearance from Leicester goalkeeper Ian Walker, who then made amends by keeping out Joseph Desire-Job's penalty. Leicester were level shortly after the restart, although Paul Dickov appeared to convert Steve Guppy's corner with his hand. Dickov put City ahead by converting Riccardo Scimeca's flick on after 65 minutes and the home side were in disarray when Marcus Bent's close-range finish made it 3-1. That was the way it stayed going into the last minute. Massimo Maccarone's goal appeared to be just a consolation for Middlesbrough, but they went on to snatch a point in the second minute of injury time through an own goal from Leicester defender John Curtis.

SATURDAY 18TH JANUARY 1997

Matt Elliott made his Leicester City debut in a 1-0 win at Wimbledon secured by Emile Heskey's goal.

TUESDAY 18TH JANUARY 2000

Joey Gudjonsson lashed home from 35 yards to secure a 1-0 win at Blackpool, and a trip to Championship rivals Reading in the fourth round of the FA Cup. The sides had battled to a 1-1 draw at the Walkers Stadium ten days earlier. Blackpool's line-up included former Leicester City skipper Simon Grayson.

WEDNESDAY 19TH JANUARY 2000

Leicester City went through to the fifth round of the FA Cup after a dramatic penalty shoot-out against Arsenal at Filbert Street. The Foxes hadn't won any of the previous ten meetings between the teams and it took several fine saves from goalkeeper Tim Flowers to keep the scoreline blank after 90 minutes to send the match into extra time. Flowers was replaced by Frenchman Pegguy Arphexad and he was City's hero in a shoot-out – that stretched to 14 kicks – saving Gilles Grimandi's kick to send City through 6-5 after Arnar Gunnlaugsson, Robbie Savage, Graham Fenton, Matt Elliott, Stuart Campbell and Emile Heskey had been on target for Martin O'Neill's team.

WEDNESDAY 19TH JANUARY 1972

Leicester City beat Wolverhampton Wanderers 2-0 in an FA Cup third round replay at Filbert Street and a crowd of 37,060 set a new record for gate receipts at the ground of £17,000. John Farrington and Len Glover got the goals.

WEDNESDAY 20TH JANUARY 1993

Julian Joachim scored a stunning solo goal at Barnsley in the FA Cup third round replay. He latched on to the ball just inside Barnsley's half, raced to the edge of the penalty area and then bent a right-footed shot into the top corner. It won the BBC's 'Goal of the Month' award, but Leicester City lost the match on penalties.

THURSDAY 20TH JANUARY 1938

Derek Dougan was born in Belfast.

SATURDAY 20TH JANUARY 2001

Roberto Mancini made his Leicester City debut in a 0-0 draw against Arsenal at Filbert Street to become the Foxes' oldest-ever debutant at the age of 36 years and 54 days old. City grabbed a point against the Gunners despite Matt Jones being sent off.

SATURDAY 20TH JANUARY 1962

Mike Stringfellow made his Leicester City debut in a 3-2 defeat at Everton. Jimmy Walsh and Howard Riley (penalty) were the Foxes' marksmen.

SATURDAY 21ST JANUARY 1961

Leicester City hammered Manchester United 6-0 in a Division One clash at Filbert Street. There were two goals apiece for Jimmy Walsh and Ken Keyworth in the romp in front of 31,308 fans. The other goals came from Gordon Wills and Howard Riley (penalty).

SATURDAY 21ST JANUARY 1989

Leicester-born goalkeeper Carl Muggleton made his Foxes debut in a 1-1 draw at West Bromwich Albion. Paul Reid grabbed City's goal in the Division Two clash.

SATURDAY 22ND JANUARY 1972

Keith Weller's stunning solo goal silenced the Trent End and sent Leicester City on their way to a 2-1 win at local rivals Nottingham Forest in Division One. Weller danced his way through several challenges before shooting home. Alan Birchenall got the other goal with Ian Storey-Moore grabbing Forest's reply.

SATURDAY 22ND JANUARY 1993

Leicester City and Notts County battled out a 1-1 draw at Filbert Street. Julian Joachim was on target for Brian Little's Leicester and the visitors' reply came from Mark Draper, who went on to play for the Foxes.

SATURDAY 22ND JANUARY 1999

Martin O'Neill's team suffered FA Cup embarrassment at Filbert Street. His Leicester City side were beaten 3-0 by Coventry City in a third round tie after two late goals.

SATURDAY 23RD JANUARY 1982

Jock Wallace's Leicester City went through to the fifth round of the FA Cup after coming away from Fourth Division Hereford United with a 1-0 win. Larry May headed home the only goal to ensure a tricky tie ended in victory and put City in to the hat for the last sixteen.

SATURDAY 23RD JANUARY 1937

Leicester City striker Jack Bowers continued his prolific form in front of goal. He scored for the sixth successive game in a 3-2 win over Plymouth Argyle that lifted the Foxes up to third in Division Two.

SATURDAY 24TH JANUARY 1920

Adam Black made the first of his 557 appearances for Leicester City in a 3-2 win over Hull City at Filbert Street. Jock Paterson (penalty), Ernie Walker and George Douglas got the City goals in a game that marked the start of a career that went on to span 15 years and 16 days.

TUESDAY 25TH JANUARY 2000

A goalless draw at Villa Park put Leicester in the driving seat in their League Cup semi-final. Aston Villa boss and former Foxes coach John Gregory suggested City had not attempted to cross the halfway line during the game, while City boss Martin O'Neill hailed a heroic performance from his side. Leicester had been hit hard by injuries and Tim Flowers made a couple of crucial saves.

WEDNESDAY 25TH JANUARY 2006

Craig Levein was sacked as Leicester City manager with the Foxes 22nd in the Championship.

WEDNESDAY 25TH JANUARY 1995

Mark Robins marked his debut for Leicester City after a £1m move from Norwich City with the only goal of the game at Premier League rivals Manchester City. The game was played in atrocious weather conditions and many supporters didn't reach Maine Road until 20 minutes before the final whistle while others didn't get there at all. Those that did make it saw Robins head home Jamie Lawrence's cross to boost Mark McGhee's team's chances of avoiding relegation. City printed a limited edition T-shirt for supporters who made it to Maine Road.

SATURDAY 25TH JANUARY 1975

A crowd of 32,090 at Filbert Street saw a classic FA Cup fourth round tie. Leicester City were 2-0 down at half-time against Isthmian League underdogs Leatherhead and only a goalline clearance prevented the Foxes falling further behind. Jon Sammels started City's second-half fightback, Steve Earle levelled the scores and Keith Weller spared the Foxes' blushes with the winning goal in a five-goal thriller.

TUESDAY 26TH JANUARY 2002

Martin O'Neill's team headed to Sunderland for the first leg of the League Cup semi-final after back-to-back drubbings at Filbert Street against Manchester United and Coventry City, by scores of 6-2 and 3-0, respectively. Sunderland were top of Division One, but Tony Cottee netted twice to hand Leicester City a 2-0 advantage going into the second leg.

SATURDAY 26TH JANUARY 1991

A 3-1 defeat at Filbert Street against Blackburn Rovers spelled the end of David Pleat's spell as manager of Leicester City. David Kelly scored City's goal and supporters protested as the Foxes crashed to a defeat that left them in deep trouble at the bottom of Division Two.

SATURDAY 27TH JANUARY 1968

Leicester City avoided being on the receiving end of an FA Cup third round upset at Colin Appleton's Barrow. Appleton was player-manager at the club in the Lake District and had inspired them to wins over Oldham Athletic and Altrincham in the previous rounds, but they were behind after three minutes against City. Frank Large's cross was turned into his own net by a Barrow defender and John Sjoberg headed home the second nine minutes after the restart before the home side pulled a goal back.

SATURDAY 27TH JANUARY 2001

Arnar Gunnlaugsson smacked home a spectacular winner to secure a 2-1 win at Aston Villa and send Leicester City through to the fifth round of the FA Cup. Ade Akinbiyi got City's opener and former Foxes striker Julian Joachim replied.

WEDNESDAY 27TH JANUARY 1943

Mike Stringfellow was born in Kirkby-in-Ashfield in Nottinghamshire.

SATURDAY 27TH JANUARY 1934

Leicester City booked their place in the fifth round of the FA Cup with a 6-3 win at Millwall. Arthur Chandler led the goal blitz with a double strike and the others came from Sep Smith, Arthur Maw, Arthur Lochhead and Danny Liddle.

SATURDAY 28TH JANUARY 1995

Iwan Roberts grabbed the only goal for Leicester City in an FA Cup fourth round tie at Portsmouth to send the Foxes through to the last sixteen.

MONDAY 28TH JANUARY 1991

David Pleat was sacked as Leicester manager with his side just above the relegation zone in Division Two.

SATURDAY 28TH JANUARY 1911

David Walker went down in the history books as the first Leicester Fosse player to ever be sent off at Filbert Street. He was dismissed in the Division Two game against Clapton Orient having earlier scored what turned out to be the winner in a 2-1 victory. Fred Shinton grabbed City's other goal.

SATURDAY 29TH JANUARY 2005

Leicester City came from behind to snatch a dramatic win at Reading in the fourth round of the FA Cup. The game was going with the form book when the Premier League Royals went ahead against their struggling visitors from the Championship with only ten minutes gone. Nicky Forster was on target and City should have fallen further behind 12 minutes later, but former Foxes striker Les Ferdinand shot wide when he had the goal at his mercy. Gareth Williams got the equaliser for the visitors on 32 minutes after smart work from David Connolly and James Scowcroft had carved open the Royals' defence. Scowcroft went on to be the Foxes' match winner in the last minute. He powered home a header from Jordan Stewart's cross to take his team through to the last 16.

SATURDAY 30TH JANUARY 1937

Leicester City suffered FA Cup embarrassment at Exeter City. The home side were locked in a battle at the bottom of Division Three (South) and sensed an upset after just ten minutes when an injury to Sep Smith meant City were left with only ten men. Exeter went on to claim a 3-1 victory with Danny Liddle on target for the Foxes.

SATURDAY 31ST JANUARY 1981

Jock Wallace's team inflicted the first home defeat on all-conquering Liverpool for 85 matches. They made the trip having lost their previous five games, but went on to topple the defending champions through goals from Pat Byrne and Jim Melrose in a 2-1 win at Anfield. Alan Young's own goal wasn't enough for the Reds to prevent City claiming a famous league double. City had been 2-0 victors when the sides clashed at Filbert Street five months earlier. The win lifted the Foxes off the bottom of the Division One table.

SATURDAY 31ST JANUARY 1998

Tony Cottee stunned Premiership leaders Manchester United with the goal that handed Leicester City their first win at Old Trafford in 17 visits. United had dropped just two Premier League points in front of their home fans that season before the game, and that all changed when Tony Cottee lifted home his first goal for the Foxes from a tight angle in the first half after latching on to Robbie Savage's pass. It was Cottee's first goal for City in just his third start for the club.

SATURDAY 31ST JANUARY 1976

Bob Lee grabbed the only goal for Leicester City in a 1-0 win over Manchester City in a Division One clash at Filbert Street. The result lifted them up to 13th in the table.

SATURDAY 31ST JANUARY 1970

Leicester City stayed ninth in Division One despite a 2-1 defeat at Watford. Len Glover was on target for the Foxes, but it wasn't enough to prevent them suffering back-to-back defeats. The result also made it four games without a win for City.

TUESDAY 31ST JANUARY 1961

Leicester City stormed through to the fifth round of the FA Cup with a 5-1 demolition of Bristol City at Filbert Street. There were two goals apiece for Ken Leek and Jimmy Walsh. Gordon Wills got the other goal.

LEICESTER CITY
On This Day

FEBRUARY

SATURDAY 1ST FEBRUARY 1986

Gordon Milne's team twice hit back after falling behind at Stamford Bridge to secure a point against Chelsea. The home side were chasing European qualification and the game was going with the form book when Duncan Shearer gave the home side the lead. Ali Mauchlen levelled for Leicester City and Steve Lynex secured a point with a 71st minute spot kick after Keith Jones had restored Chelsea's lead.

WEDNESDAY 2ND FEBRUARY 2000

Matt Elliott's header against Aston Villa at Filbert Street sent Leicester City back to Wembley for a third League Cup final in four years. Martin O'Neill's line-up included several players some way short of full fitness and they were fired up by Villa boss John Gregory's remarks about their lack of ambition in the first leg eight days earlier. Stef Oakes rattled the woodwork before Elliott headed home what proved to be the winner for the Foxes.

SATURDAY 3RD FEBRUARY 1962

David Gibson made his Leicester City debut and formed a partnership with fellow new signing Mike Stringfellow that helped inspire a 4-1 drubbing of Fulham in Division One. Fulham had been a bogey side for the Foxes in previous seasons and that looked set to continue when Johnny Haynes put the visitors ahead at Filbert Street. But Jimmy Walsh fired home the leveller for City and then a quick-fire double strike from Ken Keyworth and Howard Riley (penalty) put Leicester in charge at 3-1 ahead. Stringfellow then teed up Walsh's second to complete the scoring and end the jinx.

SATURDAY 3RD FEBRUARY 1968

Rodney Fern made his Leicester City debut in a 2-2 draw against Leeds United at Filbert Street. He was handed his chance in front of his home crowd by manager Bert Johnson, who was acting as caretaker manager during Matt Gillies' sick leave. City's scorers against Leeds were Mike Stringfellow and Frank Large.

SATURDAY 4TH FEBRUARY 1961

Leicester City became the first team to win at Tottenham Hotspur in a season that ended with the Londoners winning the Division One and FA Cup double. Jimmy Walsh was the two-goal hero for City in a 3-2 win. Ken Leek also scored.

SATURDAY 4TH FEBRUARY 1950

Leicester City stunned runaway Division Two leaders Tottenham Hotspur at White Hart Lane to give Norman Bullock's team a massive lift as they battled against the drop. There were 60,595 fans crammed inside White Hart Lane to watch the action and that remained the biggest crowd to watch Leicester until 2001. Most of them went home unhappy after goals from Charlie Adam and Bert Barlow secured maximum points for City.

SATURDAY 4TH FEBRUARY 1967

Bobby Roberts grabbed the only goal for Leicester City in a 1-0 win at Aston Villa that kept the Foxes eighth in Division One.

SATURDAY 4TH FEBRUARY 1984

Alan Smith's goal double couldn't save Leicester City from a 3-2 defeat at home to Birmingham City in Division One. Andy Peake's own goal proved to be the winner for the Blues.

SATURDAY 4TH FEBRUARY 1995

Leicester City were beaten 2-1 at home by West Ham United at Filbert Street. Mark Robins was on target for the Foxes making it two goals in as many games in the Premier League for the striker following his transfer to Filbert Street from Norwich City in a £1m deal. The defeat against the Hammers meant City stayed rooted to the foot of the table.

SATURDAY 4TH FEBRUARY 1956

Leicester City powered to a 5-1 win over Plymouth Argyle that lifted them up to third place in the Division Two table. Howard Riley and Arthur Rowley netted two goals apiece for the Foxes in the romp in front of 23,610 fans at Filbert Street and the other goal came from Jack Froggatt.

SATURDAY 5TH FEBRUARY 1972

Young goalkeeper Carl Jayes had a nightmare as Leicester City crashed out of the fourth round of the FA Cup against Jimmy Bloomfield's Leyton Orient at Filbert Street. Jayes was at fault for the second goal that took the game beyond the Foxes.

WEDNESDAY 5TH FEBRUARY 1964

Leicester City edged out West Ham United 4-3 in the first leg of the League Cup semi-final at Filbert Street. The Foxes were in charge at 4-1 through goals from Ken Keyworth, Bobby Roberts, Mike Stringfellow and Frank McLintock before the Hammers pulled two goals back with Geoff Hurst netting twice to give his side a lifeline going into the second leg the following month.

SATURDAY 5TH FEBRUARY 1983

Leicester City boss Gordon Milne had signed Gerry Daly on loan from Coventry City to boost his side's flagging hopes of gaining promotion from Division Two and he made his debut in the 1-0 win at Carlisle United. Kevin MacDonald got the only goal to spark City's promotion bid.

THURSDAY 5TH FEBRUARY 1931

Percy Richards made his Leicester City debut against Arsenal – and couldn't prevent the Gunners romping to a 7-2 win at Filbert Street. Jack Lambert bagged a hat-trick for the visitors and Cliff Bastin added a brace, while Ernie Hine grabbed both goals for the Foxes.

SATURDAY 6TH FEBRUARY 1909

Leicester Fosse bowed out of the FA Cup after a second round defeat against Derby County. The estimated crowd of 22,000 is believed to be the highest to have watched Fosse play at Filbert Street.

SUNDAY 6TH FEBRUARY 1955

Norman Bullock resigned as Leicester City manager with the Foxes in trouble near the bottom of Division One. His side had lost 2-0 at Newcastle United the previous day and an incident in a Whitley Bay hotel following the game resulted in his resignation. Johnny Morris, Bullock's main adversary, was suspended for 14 days.

SATURDAY 7TH FEBRUARY 1998

Theo Zagorakis made his Leicester City debut as a substitute against Leeds United at Filbert Street. Zagorakis was Greece's Player of the Year in 1997 and masterminded PAOK's victory over Arsenal in the Uefa Cup the following season to convince Leicester boss Martin O'Neill to sign him for £250,000 from PAOK. His debut ended with a 1-0 victory thanks to Garry Parker's penalty.

SATURDAY 8TH FEBRUARY 1964

George Best made his first visit to Filbert Street – and went home a loser. Leicester City had won five of their previous six league games and were fired up to avenge defeat against Manchester United in the FA Cup final nine months earlier. City still had nine of the cup final team in their line up, but it was Billy Hodgson, replacing the injured Howard Riley, who was the two-goal hero in a 3-2 win. Mike Stringfellow got the other and United's goals came from Denis Law and David Herd.

SATURDAY 9TH FEBRUARY 1957

David Halliday's Leicester City retained top spot in Division Two with a thrilling 3-2 win over promotion rivals Liverpool at Filbert Street. Billy Liddell and John Evans put the Merseysiders 2-0 ahead at the break and the City fightback was started by Derek Hines on 63 minutes. Arthur Rowley bagged the leveller and then buried a penalty with ten minutes left to secure a breathtaking come-from-behind victory.

FRIDAY 9TH FEBRUARY 1968

An unforgettable night at Filbert Street. Leicester City were 2-0 down inside half an hour against Manchester City in their FA Cup fourth round replay, but hit back to win 4-3 with Frank Large the two-goal hero. Rodney Fern and David Nish were the other scorers for the Foxes.

SATURDAY 9TH FEBRUARY 1935

Adam Black played the last game of a Leicester City career that included 557 appearances. But the occasion wasn't marked with a win as City were beaten 2-0 at Sunderland.

SATURDAY 10TH FEBRUARY 1973

Alan Birchenall will tell you all about his second goal against Leeds United at Filbert Street on this day if you ask him. In fact, you probably won't have to ask him! Leicester City hadn't beaten Leeds at home since 1959 and Birchenall got the breakthrough on 22 minutes when he stabbed home John Farrington's cross. His second came 11 minutes after the break and was a belter. He lashed home an unstoppable volley after Leeds goalkeeper David Harvey had saved from Frank Worthington. At the other end of the pitch, Malcolm Manley and Graham Cross performed heroics at the heart of Leicester's defence to keep out former Foxes striker Allan Clarke and Mick Jones.

SATURDAY 11TH FEBRUARY 1995

Leicester City, struggling at the bottom of the Premier League under Mark McGhee, clinched a surprise point at Arsenal. Mark Draper was on target for City and Paul Merson grabbed the Gunners' reply at Highbury.

WEDNESDAY 12TH FEBRUARY 1992

Leicester City and Nottingham Forest battled out a 1-1 draw in the first leg of the northern final of the Zenith Data Systems Cup. The prize at stake was a trip to Wembley for the final to face the winners of the southern final. Colin Gordon headed home in the second half to cancel out Scott Gemmill's opener and give Foxes' fans some cause for hope going into the second leg at the City Ground.

SATURDAY 13TH FEBRUARY 1988

Leicester City's revival under David Pleat continued with a 3-2 win over Leeds United at Filbert Street. Gary McAllister netted twice – including a penalty – and Nicky Cross got the other goal.

FRIDAY 14TH FEBRUARY 1896

Future Leicester City player and manager John Duncan was born in Lochgelly, Fife.

SATURDAY 14TH FEBRUARY 1981

Steve Lynex made his Leicester City debut in a 1-0 defeat at Sunderland after joining the Foxes from Birmingham City for £60,000.

SATURDAY 15TH FEBRUARY 1975

Leicester City held Arsenal to a goalless draw in an FA Cup fifth-round clash at Highbury. It was the fifth meeting between the sides during the season and City made the trip in confident mood having drawn previous games in North London in the league and League Cup. They had been boosted by the arrival of former Gunners defender Jeff Blockley since their last meeting and he played a major role in helping the Foxes secure a replay at Filbert Street.

SATURDAY 15TH FEBRUARY 1992

Kevin Russell was recalled to the starting line-up for the trip to Port Vale and was Leicester City's match-winner with both goals in a 2-1 win. He was on target after 11 and 68 minutes and City held on as the home side produced a grandstand finish.

SATURDAY 16TH FEBRUARY 1973

Leicester City were likened to Brazil by the national press after winning 4-0 at Luton in the fifth round of the FA Cup. Steve Earle got the first two, Frank Worthington added a third and Keith Weller completed the scoring in sensational style by dancing past several tackles on the muddy pitch and smacking an unstoppable left-foot shot into the top corner.

WEDNESDAY 17TH FEBRUARY 1999

Leicester City went into the second leg of their League Cup semi-final against Sunderland at Filbert Street leading 2-1, but were soon under pressure as Niall Quinn levelled the aggregate scores after 34 minutes. City still held the advantage on the away goals rule, but Tony Cottee eased the nerves with a 54th minute goal that followed his double strike in the first leg. Goalkeeper Kasey Keller ensured Leicester kept their advantage with a late save from Quinn.

SATURDAY 17TH FEBRUARY 1934

Arthur Chandler's two goals secured a 2-1 win at Birmingham City and sent Leicester City through to the quarter-finals of the FA Cup.

SATURDAY 18TH FEBRUARY 1898

Adam Black was born in Denny, Stirlingshire. He went on to make a club record 528 Football League appearances for Leicester City.

SATURDAY 18TH FEBRUARY 1995

Garry Parker made his Leicester City debut in an FA Cup fifth-round clash at Wolverhampton Wanderers. Parker arrived from Aston Villa and his signing helped smooth relations between the clubs following Brian Little's acrimonious departure from Filbert Street three months earlier. But his presence in midfield couldn't prevent City crashing to a 1-0 defeat at Molineux. Former Foxes striker David Kelly got the goal for the home team.

TUESDAY 18TH FEBRUARY 1997

Robert Ullathorne lasted just 11 minutes of his Leicester City debut as the Foxes battled out a goalless draw against Wimbledon in the first leg of the League Cup semi-final at Filbert Street. He was stretchered off with a broken ankle after twisting as he challenged for the ball. Emile Heskey went closest to breaking the deadlock in the game with a shot that came back off the post.

SATURDAY 18TH FEBRUARY 1928

An FA Cup fifth round clash against Tottenham Hotspur attracted a record crowd to Filbert Street. The majority of a crowd of 47,298 went home unhappy after Spurs went through to the sixth round with a 3-0 win.

SATURDAY 19TH FEBRUARY 2005

Dion Dublin's late header stunned Premiership Charlton Athletic at The Valley and sent Craig Levein's Leicester City through to the quarter-finals of the FA Cup. Leicester were on top early on and it was no surprise when Nikos Dabizas put them ahead with a 38th minute header from Danny Tiatto's cross. Charlton grabbed an equaliser in first half injury time through Shaun Bartlett. But City took the game to their hosts after the break and got their reward with just 13 seconds of normal time left when Dublin headed home to send the 4,000 travelling fans into ecstasy.

SATURDAY 20TH FEBRUARY 1999

Leicester City fielded the most cosmopolitan team in their history in the Premier League at Highbury. Martin O'Neill's starting 11 included nine different nationalities: Kasey Keller (USA), Pontus Kaamark (Sweden), Frank Sinclair (Jamaica), Matt Elliott (Scotland), Robbie Savage (Wales), Theo Zagorakis (Greece), Neil Lennon (Northern Ireland) and Arnar Gunnlaugsson (Iceland). The only Englishmen were Robert Ullathorne, Steve Guppy and Muzzy Izzet, who went on to represent Turkey. It didn't do them much good. Arsenal won 5-0.

SATURDAY 20TH FEBRUARY 1971

Goals from Rodney Fern and Malcolm Partridge secured a 2-1 win over Norwich City at Filbert Street in Division Two.

WEDNESDAY 21ST FEBRUARY 1996

Martin O'Neill took his Leicester City side to Wolverhampton Wanderers looking for his first win as Foxes manager after nine games at the helm. It proved to be worth the wait. City, fired up by playing against Mark McGhee's new team following his departure from Filbert Street two months earlier, stormed to a thrilling 3-2 win at Molineux. Emile Heskey was the two-goal hero for City – including the winner – and Iwan Roberts was also on target as Leicester kick-started their flagging promotion bid.

WEDNESDAY 21ST FEBRUARY 1934

Archie Gardiner made a stunning debut for Leicester City at Portsmouth. He bagged four goals and Danny Liddle grabbed the other in a 5-3 win at Fratton Park in the Division One clash.

SATURDAY 21ST FEBRUARY 1998

Emile Heskey got both goals for Leicester City in a 2-0 win over Chelsea at Filbert Street that lifted Martin O'Neill's team up to seventh in the Premier League. The result made it seven games unbeaten for City.

SATURDAY 21ST FEBRUARY 1981

Jock Wallace's Leicester City clinched a shock 2-1 win at Tottenham Hotspur to boost their hopes of avoiding an immediate return to Division Two. Steve Lynex and Pat Byrne were on target for the Foxes.

SATURDAY 22ND FEBRUARY 1958

Jimmy Walsh bagged four goals as Leicester City romped to an 8-4 win over Manchester City at Filbert Street. Howard Riley got two and the others came from Derek Hines and Derek Hogg.

SUNDAY 22ND FEBRUARY 2004

Leicester City and Tottenham Hotspur shared the points after an eight-goal thriller in the Premiership at White Hart Lane. The Sky Sports cameras were there to capture all the drama as ten-man Leicester battled back from 3-1 down to lead before Spurs snatched a point. Leicester fell behind when former Spurs goalkeeper Ian Walker let Michael Brown's free-kick slip through his grasp, but were level when Gary Doherty, once a transfer target for City, scooped the ball into his own net under pressure from Paul Dickov. Spurs were in charge at the break after Jermain Defoe and Robbie Keane netted to make it 3-1. The fightback started with Les Ferdinand's cool finish, but Leicester were handed a massive blow when James Scowcroft was sent off. The Foxes then stunned the home crowd by levelling. Steve Guppy's corner was powerfully headed home by former Spurs defender Ben Thatcher and incredibly, Leicester went on to snatch the lead. Dickov intercepted Doherty's back pass and Marcus Bent rolled the loose ball past former Leicester goalkeeper Kasey Keller and into the net. City couldn't hold on, however, and Defoe lashed home a late leveller via the underside of the bar.

SATURDAY 22ND FEBRUARY 2003

Leicester City fans voted against the proposal to revert to the club's original name of Leicester Fosse during the half-time interval of the 4-0 thrashing of Wimbledon. New Fox plc, the club's new owners, had made the proposal and fans were handed posters to register their vote. The overwhelming majority voted against change and City won the game 4-0 through Paul Dickov's hat-trick and Trevor Benjamin's goal to stay on course for promotion.

WEDNESDAY 22ND FEBRUARY 1995

It looked like being another miserable night in a miserable season. Leicester City fans had felt betrayed by Brian Little's departure for Aston Villa three months earlier and his new team piled on the misery at Villa Park. There appeared to be no way back for Leicester in the Premiership fixture as they trailed 4-1 with 13 minutes left. But the fightback started when Iwan Roberts headed home a Mike Galloway cross and David Lowe pulled another goal back to make it 4-3 and set up a thrilling climax. The game was deep into injury time when Lowe became the Foxes' hero by forcing home Colin Hill's header to snatch a point, giving City fans some cheer.

SATURDAY 22ND FEBRUARY 1997

Leicester City were without Muzzy Izzet, Neil Lennon and Emile Heskey for the visit of Midlands rivals Derby County to Filbert Street for a Premiership fixture. But it didn't matter. Ian Marshall scored a hat-trick in just 21 first-half minutes for the Foxes as Martin O'Neill's team hit back to win after going behind inside the opening two minutes to a goal from Dean Sturridge, who went on to play for the Foxes. Steve Claridge bagged a fourth for Leicester past former Fox Russell Hoult to complete the scoring. Derby's line-up included Gary Rowett and Jacob Laursen, who also went on to play for Leicester.

SATURDAY 23RD FEBRUARY 1963

Leicester City stayed second in Division One with a 3-0 hammering of defending champions Ipswich Town at Filbert Street. City had dumped Ipswich out of the FA Cup three weeks earlier and piled on the misery with goals from David Gibson, Mike Stringfellow and Howard Riley securing maximum points. Ken Keyworth missed out having scored in the previous six games, but it didn't matter as City boosted their title bid without his goals.

SATURDAY 24TH FEBRUARY 1996

Neil Lennon, who became Martin O'Neill's first signing when he made a £750,000 move from Crewe, made his debut in the 1-1 draw at Reading and it proved to be a memorable start for the highly-rated Northern Ireland international. He set up a goal for Neil Lewis and then conceded the penalty that enabled the Royals to earn a 1-1 draw in the Division One clash at Elm Park. Lewis never scored another goal for City.

WEDNESDAY 24TH FEBRUARY 1960

Frank McLintock, Albert Cheesebrough and Gordon Wills were the marksmen for Leicester City in a memorable 3-1 win over Manchester United at Filbert Street.

SATURDAY 24TH FEBRUARY 1934

Ken Keyworth, future City player, was born in Rotherham, Yorkshire.

MONDAY 24TH FEBRUARY 1975

The outcome of Leicester City's epic FA Cup fifth round clash against Arsenal was finally settled in extra time in the second replay at Filbert Street. John Radford rifled home a free-kick to send the Gunners through to the quarter-finals. The previous two games between the sides in the competition had ended in a goalless draw at Highbury and then a 1-1 draw at Filbert Street secured by Alan Birchenall's goal for the Foxes.

TUESDAY 24TH FEBRUARY 1981

Leicester City boss Jock Wallace revealed he had agreed terms to bring Dutch superstar Johan Cruyff to Filbert Street. Although now 33 years old, Cruyff had been rated the best player in the world and looked set to be paid between £4,000 and £5,000 per game for the remainder of the season as the Foxes battled against the drop from Division One. Wallace was convinced the payment would be recouped by an increase in attendances.

SATURDAY 25TH FEBRUARY 1984

Leicester City claimed a crucial 2-0 win over Ipswich Town at Filbert Street to boost their hopes of avoiding relegation from Division One. Alan Smith and John O'Neill got the goals.

WEDNESDAY 26TH FEBRUARY 1997

The decision to award a penalty against Leicester City in an FA Cup fifth round replay at Chelsea sparked a national outcry that prompted comment from Prime Minister and Blues fan John Major. The game was heading towards a penalty shoot-out when referee Mike Reed handed the home side a spot kick after Erland Johnsen took a tumble. Replays proved no contact had been made and Franck Leboeuf accepted the gift to put Chelsea through to the quarter-finals. The Blues went on to lift the cup at Wembley.

THURSDAY 26TH FEBRUARY 1981

Leicester City's ambitious bid to sign Johan Cruyff was called off. Foxes boss Jock Wallace got a call from Cruyff's agent saying the Dutchman was signing for Spanish club Levante after they reportedly offered him 50 per cent of gate receipts for their matches.

SATURDAY 26TH FEBRUARY 1983

Leicester City walloped Division Two promotion rivals Wolverhampton Wanderers 5-0. The game is remembered for an Alan Smith volley from 25 yards – rated by the club's programme editor as one of the most spectacular goals seen at Filbert Street for many years. Steve Lynex bagged two goals for Gordon Milne's side while Gary Lineker added another and Gerry Daly's sweetly struck shot from the edge of the penalty area completed the scoring.

WEDNESDAY 26TH FEBRUARY 1992

Leicester City were beaten 2-0 at Nottingham Forest's City Ground in the second leg of the Zenith Data Systems Cup northern final. Forest went through 3-1 on aggregate after the sides drew 1-1 at Filbert Street two weeks earlier and went on to lift the trophy at Wembley.

MONDAY 26TH FEBRUARY 1979

Leicester City crashed out of the FA Cup after defeat at Oldham Athletic in the fourth round. Future City hero Alan Young bagged a hat-trick for the Latics in a 3-1 win with Martin Henderson netting in reply for Jock Wallace's team.

SUNDAY 27TH FEBRUARY 2000

Leicester City skipper Matt Elliott lifted the League Cup at Wembley after his double strike secured a 2-1 win over Tranmere Rovers. Martin O'Neill's team were appearing in their third final in four years and went ahead against the underdogs from Division Two in the 29th minute when Elliott headed home Steve Guppy's corner. City were handed another boost on 63 minutes when Rovers defender Clint Hill was sent off for a second bookable offence after his challenge on Emile Heskey sent the Foxes striker crashing. Tranmere protested bitterly, but the ten men regrouped and stunned City by drawing level on 77 minutes through a well-taken goal from former Leicester striker David Kelly. Leicester were back in front four minutes later. Guppy supplied the cross again for Elliott to steer home his header and bring the cup back to Filbert Street for a second time in four years.

SATURDAY 28TH FEBRUARY 1925

Arthur Chandler crashed in five goals for Leicester City in a 6-0 thrashing of Barnsley in Division Two and John Duncan got the other.

SATURDAY 28TH FEBRUARY 1998

Leicester City's seven-match unbeaten run in the Premiership was ended by a 5-3 defeat at Blackburn Rovers. They gave Rovers a scare by coming back from 4-1 down to make it 4-3 before the home side added a fifth. City's goals came from Stuart Wilson, Muzzy Izzet and Robert Ullathorne.

SATURDAY 28TH FEBRUARY 1981

Steve Lynex was on target for Leicester City in a 1-1 draw against East Midlands rivals Nottingham Forest at Filbert Street, to boost the Foxes' relegation fight in Division One.

SATURDAY 28TH FEBRUARY 1953

Derek Hogg got the goal for Leicester City in a 1-1 draw against Nottingham Forest that took them up to fifth in Division Two.

SATURDAY 29TH FEBRUARY 1992

A 2-0 defeat at Millwall dented the play-off hopes of Brian Little's Leicester City.

LEICESTER CITY
On This Day

MARCH

SATURDAY 1ST MARCH 1997

Steve Guppy made his Leicester City debut in a 3-1 win at Wimbledon in the Premier League. He joined from Port Vale for a fee rising to £950,000 and moving to Filbert Street meant he was reunited with Martin O'Neill, who had worked with Guppy when he was manager of Wycombe Wanderers. Guppy's City career got off to the perfect start with three goals in the first half setting the Foxes on their way to victory. Matt Elliott netted twice for the visitors at Selhurst Park and Mark Robins added a spectacular bicycle kick.

SATURDAY 2ND MARCH 1963

Leicester City stayed second in Division One with a 2-0 win over Bill Shankly's Liverpool at Anfield. Foxes boss Matt Gillies saw goals from Ken Keyworth and David Gibson secure an eighth successive win in all competitions in front of a crowd of 54,842.

SUNDAY 3RD MARCH 1996

Steve Claridge took to the pitch at Ipswich for his Leicester City debut with his name misspelt on the back of his shirt. 'Clarridge', a £1m signing from Birmingham City, drew a blank in a game that was televised live. He must have been hoping the ink on his recently-signed contract wasn't dry as Ipswich netted three times in the opening 12 minutes of the Division One clash. Iwan Roberts gave Leicester hope with two goals – the second moments after Kevin Poole had saved a penalty at the other end – but Ian Marshall put the game beyond Martin O'Neill's team with a fourth in the dying minutes. Claridge didn't score a goal in his first six games for Leicester.

SATURDAY 3RD MARCH 1917

Leicester Fosse goalkeeper Herbert Bown got on the scoresheet in a 2-1 defeat at Hull City.

SATURDAY 3RD MARCH 1934

Arthur Chandler got the goal at Preston North End that sent Leicester City through to the semi-finals of the FA Cup.

SATURDAY 4TH MARCH 2006

An unforgettable goal from Joey Gudjonsson helped Leicester City to a 3-2 win over Hull City at the Walkers Stadium. The score was locked at 1-1 when Gudjonsson got the ball on the halfway line in the 64th minute. He looked up, spotted Hull goalkeeper Boaz Myhill off his line and launched a right-foot shot over him and into the net. Iain Hume had given the home side the lead against a team managed by former Foxes boss Peter Taylor before Hull levelled. Gudjonsson's wonder goal put Leicester back in front, but the game was heading for a draw after the Tigers levelled again. Gudjonsson grabbed the winner with seven minutes left.

SUNDAY 5TH MARCH 2000

Stan Collymore hit a terrific treble in Leicester City's 5-2 demolition of Sunderland at Filbert Street in the Premiership. Emile Heskey was also on the scoresheet and the prospect of them forming a partnership was mouth-watering for Foxes fans. It was not to be.

SATURDAY 6TH MARCH 1982

Legend has it that *Leicester Mercury* reporters in the office on the Saturday afternoon shift thought a bomb had gone off. Thankfully not. It was just the crowd cheering Leicester City's equaliser in the unforgettable FA Cup quarter-final against Shrewsbury Town. Larry May put Leicester ahead and then goalkeeper Mark Wallington was injured in a collision with Shrews striker Chic Bates. Two goals flew past Wallington while he was still groggy and Alan Young took over between the posts. Leicester were level when Shrewsbury defender Colin Griffin rolled the ball into his own net and Steve Lynex became the third Foxes players to wear the goalkeeper's jersey after Young was injured in a collision. Young returned between the posts when his head had cleared and Lynex set up Jim Melrose's goal that put Leicester ahead. Gary Lineker and Melrose added the fourth and fifth.

SATURDAY 7TH MARCH 1936

Colin Appleton was born in Scarborough. He went on to make 333 appearances for Leicester City.

SATURDAY 7TH MARCH 1981

Paul Ramsey made his Leicester City debut in a 1-0 win over Arsenal at Filbert Street. Tommy Williams got the only goal of the game in the Foxes' victory.

WEDNESDAY 8TH MARCH 1995

Emile Heskey, the promising teenage striker, made his debut in a 2-0 defeat at Queens Park Rangers in the Premiership. Heskey became the club's youngest top-flight debutant at the age of 17 years and 56 days. He was a pupil at The City of Leicester School in Evington, Leicester that was also attended by Gary Lineker.

SATURDAY 8TH MARCH 1919

Mal Griffiths was born in Merthyr Tydfil in Wales.

SATURDAY 9TH MARCH 1974

Joe Waters carved his name in Leicester City folklore with the second-half double at Queens Park Rangers that took the Foxes through to the last four of the FA Cup. Boss Jimmy Bloomfield handed the young Irishman his chance in the absence of Alan Birchenall and Alan Woollett and he put City ahead with a strike that was later voted 'Goal of the Month'. Waters added a second minutes later – coolly clipping his shot past the advancing goalkeeper – and Leicester were through to the semi-finals. But they had been under fire for much of the first half and were relieved to reach the half-time interval on level terms.

TUESDAY 9TH MARCH 1982

Mark Wallington's run of 331 consecutive appearances in goal for Leicester City came to an end. The injury suffered in the thrilling FA Cup quarter-final win over Shrewsbury Town at Filbert Street three days earlier ruled him out of the trip to Chelsea in Division Two. He was replaced between the posts by Nicky Walker and City were beaten 4-1. The Foxes goal came from Steve Lynex.

EMILE HESKEY

SATURDAY 10TH MARCH 2001

Leicester City were on the receiving end of an FA Cup upset as Second Division Wycombe Wanderers grabbed a dramatic 2-1 win at Filbert Street in their quarter-final clash. Wycombe had been so short of players in the countdown to the clash that they advertised on the internet and that led to striker Roy Essandoh being recruited on a two-week trial. He went on to head home the injury-time winner that stunned Filbert Street. Paul McCarthy had put Wycombe ahead in the second half before Muzzy Izzet equalised, but City's goalscorer and Robbie Savage were injured and Leicester unravelled. Wycombe boss Lawrie Sanchez was dismissed from the touchline after questioning the officials and he watched on a television monitor as Essandoh rose unchallenged to head home the winner. This defeat kick-started a club record spell of nine straight losses for Peter Taylor's team.

FRIDAY 10TH MARCH 2000

Emile Heskey left Leicester City to join Liverpool in an £11m deal – five days after joining forces with Stan Collymore to fire the Foxes to a 5-2 win over Sunderland.

TUESDAY 11TH MARCH 1997

Simon Grayson's header in the League Cup semi-final, second leg at Wimbledon sent Leicester City through to Wembley. He netted the equaliser after Marcus Gayle had put the Dons ahead at Selhurst Park. The game went into extra time and Garry Parker made two goal-line clearances to ensure Leicester won on the away goals rule.

SATURDAY 11TH MARCH 1972

Mark Wallington made his Leicester City debut and kept a clean sheet in the 2-0 win over West Ham United at Filbert Street.

WEDNESDAY 11TH MARCH 1992

Leicester City striker Paul Kitson joined Derby County in a £1.35m move that involved Phil Gee and Ian Ormondroyd making the move in the opposite direction.

TUESDAY 11TH MARCH 1958

John O'Neill was born in Derry, Northern Ireland.

SATURDAY 12TH MARCH 1960

Len Chalmers' own goal ended Leicester City's hopes of securing a place in the semi-finals of the FA Cup. He scored what proved to be the winner for Wolverhampton Wanderers in the sixth-round tie at Filbert Street. The visitors went through 2-1 with Tommy McDonald grabbing City's goal.

SATURDAY 12TH MARCH 1994

Brian Little's Leicester City climbed to second place in Division One with a 2-0 victory over Middlesbrough at Filbert Street. Julian Joachim and David Speedie were on target.

SATURDAY 12TH MARCH 1949

Leicester City grabbed a 3-3 draw at Bradford Park Avenue to make it 12 games without defeat. But the Foxes gleaned only eight league points from the unbeaten spell to remain in trouble at the bottom of Division Two. Don Revie netted twice at Bradford with Jack Lee also on target.

SUNDAY 13TH MARCH 2005

Former Leicester City striker Paul Dickov broke Foxes' hearts in the FA Cup quarter-final against Premiership Blackburn Rovers at Ewood Park. Dickov netted from the penalty spot with just eight minutes left after City defender Darren Kenton sent Morten Gamst Pedersen crashing in the box. City's protests were waved away and a run that had proved a welcome distraction from the struggles in the Championship came to a controversial end. David Thompson had rattled Leicester's woodwork with a third-minute free kick, but the visitors came back and Joey Gudjonsson and Mark De Vries went close before Dickov struck.

WEDNESDAY 13TH MARCH 1912

Septimus Smith, regarded as one of Leicester City's greatest-ever players, was born in Whitburn, County Durham.

SATURDAY 14TH MARCH 1992

Simon Grayson made his Leicester City debut in a 0-0 draw at Ipswich Town that is also remembered for Ian Ormondroyd having two goals ruled out in the first half.

MONDAY 15TH MARCH 1965

Leicester City ended the first leg of their League Cup Final against Chelsea trailing 3-2. Eddie McCreadie's spectacular goal gave the Pensioners the advantage at Stamford Bridge. Colin Appleton and Jimmy Goodfellow got the goals for City to give them a fighting chance going into the second leg.

MONDAY 15TH MARCH 1971

Leicester City were left fuming by defeat at Arsenal in an FA Cup sixth-round replay at Highbury. Rodney Fern had a header controversially chalked off for a push and then Charlie George grabbed the game's only goal to send the Gunners through to the semi-finals.

SATURDAY 15TH MARCH 1980

Paul Edmunds grabbed his first goal for Leicester City in a 2-0 win over Shrewsbury Town to keep the Foxes in the hunt for promotion from Division Two. Alan Young got the other goal for the Foxes.

SATURDAY 16TH MARCH 1957

Arthur Rowley blasted home the winner at Swansea Town to take Dave Halliday's Foxes eight points clear of Nottingham Forest at the top of Division Two. Derek Hines put Leicester City ahead after only four minutes, but Des Palmer's double put the home side ahead at the interval. Ian McNeil drew Leicester level six minutes after the restart and the winner came with 15 minutes left to keep City on course for promotion to the top flight.

SATURDAY 17TH MARCH 1934

Leicester City's FA Cup semi-final against Portsmouth attracted a crowd of 66,544 to Birmingham City's St Andrew's ground. They saw City's Sep Smith line up against brothers Jack and Willie, but it was Pompey striker John Weddle who took the headlines with a hat-trick that fired his side to a 4-1 win. Arthur Lochhead got City's goal in the first half, but the defence struggled to cope after Sandy Wood was left dazed following a collision with a touchline photographer that left him with a broken nose.

WEDNESDAY 18TH MARCH 1959

Leicester City's match against Birmingham City was the first midweek game to be played under floodlights at Filbert Street. City were beaten 4-2 in the Division Two fixture with Jimmy Walsh grabbing both goals for the Foxes.

SATURDAY 19TH MARCH 1975

Leicester City drew 1-1 with Liverpool at Filbert Street in Division One. Frank Worthington was on target for City and John Toshack replied for the Reds. Toshack had been on the brink of joining the Foxes four months earlier in a £160,000 deal. The Welsh striker trained with City before a medical query led to the deal falling through.

SATURDAY 19TH MARCH 1966

Mike Stringfellow got the only goal against Sheffield United at Filbert Street to lift Leicester City back into the top ten in Division One. The win took them to ninth in the table.

THURSDAY 20TH MARCH 1952

Steve Whitworth was born in Ellistown, Leicestershire

SUNDAY 21ST MARCH 1999

Leicester City suffered heartbreak in the League Cup Final against Tottenham Hotspur at Wembley. Allan Nielsen headed home from close range in injury time to take the trophy back to White Hart Lane. Leicester were playing against ten men from the 63rd minute following the dismissal of Spurs midfielder Justin Edinburgh who was sent off after a clash with Robbie Savage. There were few chances in the game and City came closest to breaking the deadlock before the late drama when Spurs defender Ramon Vega denied Emile Heskey a shot at goal with a last-ditch challenge.

WEDNESDAY 21ST MARCH 1979

Steve Whitworth made his 400th and last appearance for Leicester City. They beat Fulham 1-0 at Filbert Street through a Dave Buchanan goal and Whitworth went on to join Sunderland later in the month.

SATURDAY 22ND MARCH 1975

Chris Garland grabbed all the goals for Leicester City in their 3-2 win over Wolverhampton Wanderers at Filbert Street that secured two priceless points in the battle against relegation from Division One.

SATURDAY 23RD MARCH 1957

Jimmy Walsh made his debut in a 3-1 defeat at home to Fulham after joining from Celtic.

SATURDAY 23RD MARCH 1963

A club-record run of ten straight wins in all competitions had taken Matt Gillies' Leicester City up to second place in Division One and set up a top-of-the-table clash against leaders Tottenham Hotspur at Filbert Street. Fans started queuing hours before kick-off and the gates were shut with 41,622 fans crammed inside to watch a match billed as a possible championship decider. Mike Stringfellow put Leicester ahead, but Bobby Smith and Jimmy Greaves replied. City were relieved when the referee blew his whistle for half-time seconds before Greaves put the ball in the net for what would have been a crucial third goal. They made the most of the reprieve with Ken Keyworth grabbing a second-half equaliser.

THURSDAY 23RD MARCH 1961

The FA Cup semi-final replay between Leicester City and Sheffield United at the City Ground ended goalless after extra time. That meant the two sides had failed to produce a goal in three and a half hours of forgettable football.

MONDAY 23RD MARCH 1964

Leicester City went to West Ham United for the second leg of the League Cup semi-final with a 4-3 lead and goals from Frank McLintock and Bobby Roberts secured a 2-0 win at Upton Park that took the Foxes through to the final.

TUESDAY 23RD MARCH 1993

Leicester City made it six successive wins in Division One (second tier) with a 3-1 victory at Cambridge United's Abbey Stadium. David Lowe was on target twice for the Foxes after Julian Joachim had opened the scoring for the Foxes.

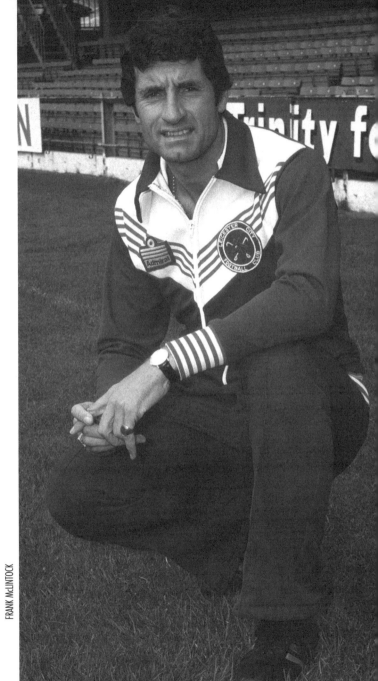

FRANK McLINTOCK

SATURDAY 24TH MARCH 1956

Leicester City stayed second in Division Two despite a 6-1 defeat at promotion rivals Swansea Town. Jack Froggatt grabbed the consolation goal for the Foxes. Incredibly, City had won by the same margin when the sides had clashed at Filbert Street four months earlier in the season.

SATURDAY 24TH MARCH 1990

David Pleat's Leicester City had received a double boost two days before the Division Two clash against Plymouth Argyle at Filbert Street. Gary McAllister turned down a deadline day move to Nottingham Forest and Republic of Ireland striker David Kelly joined from West Ham United for £300,000. Kelly impressed on his debut and McAllister gave City the lead with a penalty after 27 minutes. Plymouth secured a point in their battle against the drop when Nicky Marker equalised 12 minutes after the restart.

FRIDAY 24TH MARCH 1967

Leicester City ended a run of three games without a win at Manchester City. They ran out 3-1 winners to claim their first win at Maine Road since 1930 and climb to seventh in Division One and boost their chances of securing qualification for Europe. The first three goals all came from the penalty spot with the home side going ahead after Richie Norman's handball. City were level three minutes after the restart. Jackie Sinclair netted from the penalty spot after he had been up-ended and scored another spot kick on 61 minutes to put the Foxes ahead after a foul on Paul Matthews. Mike Stringfellow put the game beyond the home side by turning home City's third from a David Gibson free kick.

SATURDAY 25TH MARCH 1989

Ali Mauchlen bagged both goals for Leicester City in a 2-0 win over Birmingham City in Division Two in front of 9,564 fans at Filbert Street. The result made it three games unbeaten for David Pleat's team and kept them 15th in the table.

TUESDAY 26TH MARCH 1985

Gary Lineker grabbed the first of his 48 goals for England in a friendly against the Republic of Ireland at Wembley. His goal proved to be the winner in a 2-1 victory. Trevor Steven put England ahead on the stroke of half-time and then Lineker struck on 76 minutes after being set up by substitute Peter Davenport. Liam Brady pulled a goal back for the visitors in the 87th minute.

SATURDAY 26TH MARCH 1977

Larry May made his Leicester City debut in a 0-0 draw against Bristol City in Division One as an 18-year-old.

MONDAY 27TH MARCH 1961

Goals from Jimmy Walsh and Ken Leek secured victory over Sheffield United in their second FA Cup semi-final replay at St Andrew's and took Leicester City through to face Division One champions Tottenham Hotspur at Wembley. The previous two meetings had failed to produce a goal, but there was more drama this time. Ian King had a penalty saved after 11 minutes before Walsh headed Leicester into the lead to end a run of 451 minutes without a goal. Leek added a second just after the interval and the Blades were handed a lifeline on 65 minutes when they were awarded a spot kick. But Graham Shaw shot wide and City were on their way to Wembley.

FRIDAY 27TH MARCH 1992

Northern Ireland international Colin Hill made his Leicester City debut after arriving on loan from Sheffield United in a 2-1 win at Tranmere Rovers in Division One. Ian Ormondroyd got City's opener and Phil Gee thumped home a spectacular winner.

SATURDAY 27TH MARCH 1993

Leicester City's 3-1 win over Charlton Athletic at Filbert Street set a club record of seven successive league wins. Steve Walsh bagged two goals and Julian Joachim the other in a win that kept Brian Little's team on course for promotion to the Premier League.

SATURDAY 28TH MARCH 1953

Tom Dryburgh netted for Leicester City after just ten seconds of their Division Two clash against Swansea Town and Johnny Morris got the Foxes' other goal in a 2-1 victory.

SATURDAY 29TH MARCH 1969

Steve Guppy was born in Winchester, Hampshire.

SATURDAY 30TH MARCH 1996

I'll keep this brief. A section of Leicester City fans protested and some called for manager Martin O'Neill to be sacked after a 2-0 defeat at home to Sheffield United in Division One. Muzzy Izzet made his debut in midfield after joining on loan from Chelsea and Julian Watts also made his first start for the Foxes. Watts' partner at the heart of defence was Brian Carey, who never played for Leicester again.

SATURDAY 30TH MARCH 1974

Leicester City took on Liverpool in the FA Cup semi-final at Old Trafford. Jimmy Bloomfield's team had set pulses racing with wins at Luton Town and Queens Park Rangers in the previous rounds and might have hoped to draw either Newcastle United or Burnley in the last four. Instead, they faced Liverpool in what turned out to be a disappointing spectacle. The Reds had more possession, but hard work from Leicester defenders Malcolm Munro and Graham Cross kept clear-cut chances to a minimum in front of a crowd of 60,000 in Manchester. The best chance of the match fell to Liverpool striker Kevin Keegan in the dying minutes and he shot against the post when it looked easier to score to ensure the game went to a replay.

SATURDAY 30TH MARCH 1957

Ian McNeill scored after just ten seconds of Leicester City's Division Two clash at local rivals Nottingham Forest. Derek Hines got the other goal in a 2-1 win for the Foxes. The win kept City on top of the table and was the perfect response to the 3-1 defeat at home to Fulham seven days earlier.

TUESDAY 31ST MARCH 1981

Jock Wallace's City battled to a 3-3 draw at Manchester City in Division One., with goals from Tommy Williams, Alan Young and Jim Melrose.

LEICESTER CITY
On This Day

APRIL

MONDAY 1ST APRIL 1969

April Fools' Day – and the joke was on Leicester City. They travelled to local rivals Coventry City for a crucial relegation battle and were on course for a point with seven minutes left with the score goalless. City looked set to make the breakthrough when they were awarded a penalty after Brian Greenhalgh was scythed down, but the referee changed his mind after consulting his linesman and the Sky Blues made the most of the reprieve. They raced away to the other end of the pitch and Neil Martin scored what proved to be the winner.

TUESDAY 2ND APRIL 1996

Steve Claridge grabbed his first goal for Leicester City in a 1-0 win at Charlton Athletic that launched Martin O'Neill's team's charge for the Division One play-off places.

SATURDAY 2ND APRIL 1949

Leicester City battled to a 1-1 draw against Grimsby Town in Division Two and there was heartbreak for Foxes goalkeeper Ian McGraw. He suffered a hand injury that kept him out of the FA Cup Final against Wolverhampton Wanderers at Wembley four weeks later. Ken Chisholm got the goal for City against the Mariners.

SATURDAY 3RD APRIL 1982

Leicester City suffered FA Cup semi-final heartbreak against Tottenham Hotspur at Villa Park. Jock Wallace's Second Division underdogs were beaten by a Garth Crooks strike and midfielder Ian Wilson's own goal. City defender Tommy Williams suffered a broken leg.

SATURDAY 3RD APRIL 1954

Leicester City climbed back up to second in Division Two with a 1-0 win over Bristol Rovers at Filbert Street. Jack Froggatt got the winner for the Foxes in front of 27,369 fans.

SATURDAY 4TH APRIL 1959

Jimmy Walsh was Leicester City's two-goal hero in front of 40,795 fans at Filbert Street. Walsh grabbed both the Foxes' goals in a 2-1 win over Aston Villa that secured two precious points in the battle against relegation from Division One.

TUESDAY 5TH APRIL 1998

Leicester City and Derby County fought out a thrilling 3-3 draw at Filbert Street – and all six goals came in a 29-minute spell. Iwan Roberts bagged a hat-trick for Leicester and former Foxes striker Paul Kitson got two for the visitors.

SATURDAY 5TH APRIL 2003

Micky Adams' Leicester City team took another step towards promotion from Division One with a 2-0 win over Grimsby Town at the Walkers Stadium. Trevor Benjamin and Callum Davidson were the marksmen for the Foxes.

MONDAY 5TH APRIL 1965

There was League Cup Final heartbreak for Leicester City at Filbert Street. They went into the second leg against Chelsea trailing 3-2 to a side that boasted stars such as Bonetti, Harris, McCreadie, Tambling, Bridges and Venables. Bobby Roberts had an early effort for the home side smothered and Leicester were well on top throughout. But they couldn't find a way through and the trophy that they had won 12 months earlier was held aloft by Terry Venables in front of the directors' box.

WEDNESDAY 5TH APRIL 1978

Frank McLintock was sacked as Leicester City manager with the Foxes heading for relegation from Division One.

SATURDAY 5TH APRIL 1958

Arthur Rowley and Howard Riley bagged two goals apiece in a 5-3 win over Aston Villa at Filbert Street that handed Leicester City a boost in their battle against relegation from Division One.

SUNDAY 5TH APRIL 2004

Leicester City's hopes of staying in the Premier League were handed a hammer blow at Leeds United in front of the Sky Sports cameras. They battled back from 2-0 down to level through goals from Paul Dickov and Muzzy Izzet, but a late winner from Alan Smith handed victory to Leeds and left the Foxes in deep trouble.

SUNDAY 6TH APRIL 1997

Emile Heskey bundled home a late equaliser against Middlesbrough to force a replay in the League Cup Final. The sides had met at Filbert Street three weeks earlier and Brazilian Juninho inspired the visitors to a 3-1 win. Fearing a repeat, Leicester City boss Martin O'Neill handed Swedish international Pontus Kaamark the job of shackling Middlesbrough's little playmaker. He did just that, but nobody could stop Italian striker Fabrizio Ravanelli firing 'Boro into the lead in extra time. Heskey came to Leicester's rescue with three minutes left.

SATURDAY 6TH APRIL 1957

Leicester City took a step towards clinching promotion to Division One with a 5-3 win over West Ham United. Arthur Rowley was the goal hero with his fourth hat-trick of the season and the others came from Billy Wright.

SATURDAY 6TH APRIL 2002

Leicester City were beaten 1-0 at home by Manchester United and relegated from the Premier League in what proved to be Dave Bassett's last game in charge. The Foxes had been booked for the drop for several weeks and it was confirmed by Ole Gunnar Solskjaer's 62nd minute goal. It ended the Foxes' six-year stay in the top flight.

SATURDAY 7TH APRIL 1993

Steve Walsh was the last-gasp goal hero in a 2-1 win over Oxford United at Filbert Street that made it nine games unbeaten for Brian Little's team and Richard Smith took the plaudits at the other end of the pitch. Smith went between the posts after Carl Muggleton was injured in the second half and he kept out Oxford. City's other goal came from Steve Thompson's first-half penalty that opened the scoring. Muggleton never played for Leicester again.

TUESDAY 7TH APRIL 1953

Arthur Rowley bagged his 100th goal for Leicester City in his 122nd appearance for the club. He got two goals in a 3-2 win over Rotherham United in Division Two.

MONDAY 8TH APRIL 1963

Leicester City drew 1-1 at Blackpool and went top of Division One for the first time since September 1927. Ken Keyworth got City's goal.

MONDAY 8TH APRIL 2002

Micky Adams took over as Leicester City manager having been assistant to Dave Bassett. The Foxes were already relegated from the Premier League when Adams was appointed.

SATURDAY 9TH APRIL 1966

Mike Stringfellow got both goals for Leicester City in a memorable 2-1 win at Manchester United in Division One. The result took the Foxes up to seventh in the top flight.

WEDNESDAY 9TH APRIL 1975

Leicester City's relegation fears in Division One were eased by a 1-0 win over Middlesbrough at Filbert Street. Frank Worthington got the goal.

SATURDAY 9TH APRIL 1994

Brian Little's Leicester City team kept the pressure on the top two teams in Division One with a 3-2 win over Sunderland at Roker Park. Julian Joachim netted twice and on-loan midfielder Paul Kerr got the other from the penalty spot.

SATURDAY 10TH APRIL 1897

Willie Freebairn became the first Leicester Fosse player to ever be sent off. Freebairn got his marching orders in the 2-1 defeat at Lincoln City having earlier scored Fosse's goal.

SATURDAY 10TH APRIL 1937

Leicester City's clash with Aston Villa attracted a then-record crowd of 39,127 to Filbert Street and they saw Foxes striker Jack Bowers grab the game's only goal. The result kept the Foxes second in Division Two with three games of the season left.

SATURDAY 11TH APRIL 1987

Leicester City and relegation rivals Aston Villa battled out a 1-1 draw at Filbert Street in Division One. Steve Moran was the marksman for City.

SATURDAY 12TH APRIL 1980

Jock Wallace's team struck a crucial blow in the battle for promotion from Division Two with a 2-1 win over Birmingham City at Filbert Street that took them up to second place. Wallace raised a few eyebrows with his decision to leave out Gary Lineker, bring in Geoff Scott at full-back and move Bobby Smith forward, but he was vindicated by two goals inside the opening half-hour. Ian Wilson lashed home from 30 yards after just ten minutes and Scott crossed for Alan Young to double the lead with a header on 28 minutes. Leicester City stayed on top, but had to endure a tense final 11 minutes after John O'Neill's handball gifted the visitors the chance to halve the arrears from the penalty spot.

SATURDAY 12TH APRIL 1969

Leicester City's Division One survival hopes were dealt a massive blow by a 2-1 defeat against Liverpool at Filbert Street. Peter Rodrigues got City's goal in front of 28,671, but the visitors went away with both points courtesy of goals from Emlyn Hughes and Ian Callaghan.

MONDAY 12TH APRIL 1971

Rodney Fern masterminded a 3-1 win at Luton Town that extended Leicester City's unbeaten run to 11 games, kept them on top of Division Two and dented the Hatters' promotion ambitions. Leicester went into the game having not conceded a goal for four games and that run was ended just two minutes into the game when John Sjoberg turned the ball into his own net. City stormed back with Fern the architect. Malcolm Manley headed an equaliser just before the break, John Farrington fired home a free-kick on the hour and Ally Brown added a third.

TUESDAY 12TH APRIL 1966

Goals from Tom Sweenie and Jackie Sinclair lifted Leicester City up to sixth in the Division One table. It was a third straight victory for Matt Gillies' team.

SATURDAY 13TH APRIL 1991

Leicester City's hopes of avoiding what would have been a first-ever drop into the third tier of English football looked bleak after a 2-1 defeat at relegation rivals West Bromwich Albion. Don Goodman grabbed the winner in the last minute for the Baggies. The game had started well for Leicester with Kevin Russell putting them ahead after just two minutes. Former Foxes striker Winston White levelled just before the break and then Goodman had the final word with the winning goal.

SATURDAY 13TH APRIL 2002

Micky Adams started his spell in charge of Leicester City with a 2-2 draw at Everton in the Premier League. The Foxes were on course for maximum points when Brian Deane netted twice in the first half to put them 2-0 ahead at the interval. They were denied victory by Darren Ferguson's 86th minute equaliser after Nick Chadwick had halved the arrears for the Toffeemen.

TUESDAY 14TH APRIL 2001

Leicester City and Southampton shared the points and six goals after a thriller at The Dell. The home side led 2-1 at the break with Egil Ostenstad netting twice and Neil Lennon rifling home from 25 yards in reply. David Hirst put the Saints two goals clear four minutes after the interval, but Matt Elliott handed Leicester a lifeline three minutes later. The leveller came deep into injury time. There was a handball in Southampton's penalty area and Garry Parker crashed home the resulting spot kick.

SATURDAY 14TH APRIL 1956

Mal Griffiths made his last appearance for Leicester City against West Ham United at Filbert Street. He was on target in the 2-1 win with Willie Gardiner grabbing City's other goal. Griffiths made a total of 420 appearances for the Foxes and was the first Leicester player to score at Wembley. He got City's goal in the 1949 FA Cup final defeat against Wolverhampton Wanderers.

WEDNESDAY 15TH APRIL 1964

Davie Gibson's chip from 20 yards meant honours were even after the first leg of the League Cup Final with Stoke City going into the second leg at Filbert Street seven days later.

SATURDAY 15TH APRIL 1989

On the same day as the Hillsborough tragedy when 96 fans died at the FA Cup semi-final between Liverpool and Nottingham Forest, Leicester City ended Chelsea's 27-match unbeaten record with a 2-0 Division Two win at Filbert Street. Paul Reid put David Pleat's team in front and Nicky Cross forced home the second from close range.

SATURDAY 15TH APRIL 1995

A 4-0 defeat against Manchester United meant Leicester City were relegated from the Premiership. Andy Cole got two goals for the Reds.

TUESDAY 16TH APRIL 1997

Martin O'Neill's heroes brought major silverware back to Filbert Street for the first time since 1964 after a 1-0 win over Middlesbrough at Hillsborough in their League Cup Final replay. Steve Claridge was the Foxes' hero again. He hooked home the only goal in extra time after Steve Walsh had headed down Garry Parker's free-kick and goalkeeper Kasey Keller came to Leicester City's rescue moments later with a crucial save. The win secured the Foxes' place in the following season's Uefa Cup.

SATURDAY 16TH APRIL 1983

Gary Lineker was on target twice in a 3-1 win over Rotherham United at Filbert Street and that meant he became the first Leicester City player since Arthur Rowley in 1957 to score 25 goals in a season.

SATURDAY 16TH APRIL 1892

Leicester Fosse were hammered 11-0 at Rotherham Town in the Midland League. Horace Bailey was Fosse's under-fire goalkeeper.

SATURDAY 16TH APRIL 1963

Ken Keyworth bagged a hat-trick in just six minutes in Leicester City's thrilling 4-3 win over Manchester United in Division One. Terry Heath got the other goal and Denis Law grabbed a treble for the visitors.

SATURDAY 17TH APRIL 1971

Leicester City stayed top of Division Two with a goalless draw at Sunderland. The result stretched their unbeaten run to 14 games.

SATURDAY 18TH APRIL 1970

A 2-1 win over Queens Park Rangers at Filbert Street wasn't enough to secure promotion for Leicester City to Division One. They finished third in the table after goals from David Nish and Ally Brown ensured victory over Rangers.

FRIDAY 19TH APRIL 1957

A 5-1 win at Leyton Orient secured the Division Two title. Debutant Jimmy Moran got on the scoresheet as Leicester City enjoyed a goal romp in the spring sunshine with Arthur Rowley and Derek Hines also on target. Orient defender Facey is credited with two own goals by some sources, but Leicester gave the opening goal to Billy Wright.

SATURDAY 19TH APRIL 2003

A crowd of 31,909 at the Walkers Stadium saw Micky Adams' Leicester City secure promotion to the Premier League with a 2-0 win over Brighton & Hove Albion. Muzzy Izzet put the Foxes on course for victory with a glancing header from Paul Dickov's cross after just ten minutes and the lead was doubled just before the break. Izzet was the provider with a cross that Jordan Stewart powerfully headed into the roof of the net. That was enough to clinch maximum points and spark scenes of wild celebration at the final whistle.

SATURDAY 19TH APRIL 1975

Mike Stringfellow played his last game for Leicester City in the 0-0 draw against East Midlands rivals Derby County at Filbert Street in Division One. Stringfellow made a total of 370 appearances for the Foxes and bagged 97 goals.

MONDAY 19TH APRIL 1954

Leicester City's 4-0 win over Blackburn Rovers took the Foxes to the brink of promotion to Division One. Arthur Rowley and Johnny Morris shared the goals at Filbert Street in front of a new record crowd of 40,047.

SATURDAY 20TH APRIL 1981

Leicester City were left in deep trouble at the bottom of Division One after a 2-1 defeat at relegation rivals Brighton & Hove Albion. An ill-tempered game burst into life in the 40th minute when Jim Melrose had a goal disallowed. Two minutes later Alan Young was sent off following a second bookable offence. Leicester still went ahead before the break courtesy of Kevin MacDonald's header, but two goals in the space of four second-half minutes powered the Seagulls to victory. The result proved to be crucial at the end of the season with Brighton staying up and Leicester being relegated.

SATURDAY 20TH APRIL 1935

There was controversy as Leicester City slipped deeper into relegation trouble in Division One following a 1-1 draw at Sheffield Wednesday. Sandy Wood broke his collarbone and City were left fuming after the referee ruled that Tony Carroll's shot had not crossed the line when the scores were locked at 1-1. Gene O'Callaghan netted the goal for the Foxes.

WEDNESDAY 21ST APRIL 1909

Leicester Fosse were humiliated 12-0 at Nottingham Forest and an investigation revealed that the players may have been suffering after spending the previous day celebrating the marriage of former team mate 'Leggy' Turner. The *Leicester Chronicle* reported: "Fosse have taken a good many beatings in their time, but they have never before participated in such a farcically absurd game."

WEDNESDAY 21ST APRIL 1999

Emile Heskey was ruled out of the game at Liverpool through illness, Ian Marshall stepped in and was the last-gasp goal hero. He was on target in injury time to ensure Leicester City stretched their unbeaten run to seven games.

SATURDAY 21ST APRIL 1926

A bad day for goalkeepers. Arthur Rowley was born in Wolverhampton and he went on to become the Football League's record goalscorer and is second only to Arthur Chandler in City's goalscoring charts.

MONDAY 22ND APRIL 1957

A 4-1 defeat at home to Leyton Orient didn't spoil the celebrations at Filbert Street as Leicester City were crowned Division Two champions in front of 27,582 fans. Billy Wright got the goal for City. Arthur Rowley finished the season with 44 goals and that haul included four hat-tricks.

SATURDAY 22ND APRIL 1967

Alan Woollett made his Leicester City debut as a substitute in the 2-2 draw against Sheffield United in Division One that was secured by goals from Mike Stringfellow and Bobby Roberts. He went on to make a total of 260 appearances for his home-town club.

WEDNESDAY 22ND APRIL 1964

Leicester City got their hands on their first major trophy after beating Stoke City in the second leg of the League Cup Final at Filbert Street in front of a crowd of 25,372. The scores were locked at 1-1 after the first leg seven days earlier and Mike Stringfellow put Leicester ahead in the return with just six minutes on the clock. David Gibson's header restored the lead after the visitors levelled and Leicester had one hand on the trophy when Howard Riley put them 3-1 ahead on the night and 4-2 in front on aggregate. Stoke pulled one back in injury time to set up a tense climax, but Leicester hung on and jubilant skipper Colin Appleton lifted the trophy.

MONDAY 22ND APRIL 1935

Arthur Chandler played the last game of his record-breaking Leicester City career in the 2-2 draw against Grimsby Town at Filbert Street. Danny Liddle got both goals for City. Chandler remains City's record goalscorer. He found the target an astonishing 273 times in 419 appearances.

SATURDAY 23RD APRIL 1983

Ian Wilson's shot bobbled its way into Fulham's net and Leicester City folklore at Craven Cottage to strike a crucial blow in the battle for promotion to Division One.

TUESDAY 24TH APRIL 1979

Gary Lineker's first goal for Leicester City gave Jock Wallace's team a 1-0 win at Notts County in Division Two. He went on to score 102 more goals for his home-town club.

SATURDAY 24TH APRIL 1954

A 3-1 win at Brentford took Norman Bullock's team to the Second Division championship. Mal Griffiths, John Morris and an own goal powered Leicester City to victory.

SATURDAY 24TH APRIL 1937

Leicester City secured promotion to Division One with a 2-1 win against East Midlands rivals Nottingham Forest at Filbert Street. Jack Bowers and Arthur Maw got the goals for City in front of a crowd of 24,267 and their hopes of securing the championship were boosted by promotion rivals Blackpool being held to a 1-1 draw by bottom team Doncaster Rovers. That meant the battle for top spot went into the final day of the season.

SATURDAY 24TH APRIL 2004

Paul Dickov's missed penalty against former club Manchester City at the Walkers Stadium left Leicester City in deep trouble at the bottom of the Premier League. Both sides were desperate for points and the visitors went ahead in front of a sell-out crowd of 31,457 late in the first half through Michael Trabant's goal. James Scowcroft drew the Foxes level and they looked set to claim maximum points after being awarded an 81st minute spot kick after Trabant sent Muzzy Izzet crashing. Dickov's shot from 12 yards was kept out by David James to strike a massive blow to Micky Adams' team's hopes of avoiding an instant return to the Championship following the previous campaign's promotion.

SATURDAY 25TH APRIL 1925

George Carr got the only goal for Leicester City against Bradford City at Filbert Street to secure promotion from Division Two in front of 25,000 fans. Reg Osborne had earlier missed a penalty – City's fifth miss in nine attempts during the season – but it didn't matter.

SATURDAY 26TH APRIL 1969

A third FA Cup Final in the 1960s – and fourth in total – ended in more heartbreak. Leicester City were led by David Nish – at 21-years-old the youngest ever FA Cup Final captain – and his team were beaten by Neil Young's 23rd minute goal. Peter Rodrigues, Allan Clarke and Andy Lochhead went close to a leveller, but it never came and an eight-year-old Gary Lineker cried all the way back home to Leicester.

SUNDAY 26TH APRIL 1998

Leicester City stunned Derby at Pride Park with a four-goal blitz inside the opening 15 minutes. Emile Heskey and Muzzy Izzet put City in charge inside three minutes and Heskey and Ian Marshall added the others.

SATURDAY 26TH APRIL 2008

Leicester City were on the brink of relegation to the third tier of English football for the first time in their history after relegation rivals Sheffield Wednesday left the Walkers Stadium with a 3-1 win. Ian Holloway's team knew victory would secure survival and Iain Hume gave them an early lead. There were more celebrations when City goalkeeper Paul Henderson kept out Deon Burton's spot kick. But a goal late in the first half from Bartosz Slusarski drew Wednesday level and Leicester fell apart after the break. Steve Watson put the visitors ahead, Hume missed a penalty and Leon Clarke bagged a late third.

SATURDAY 26TH APRIL 1958

Leicester City travelled to Birmingham City needing a point to avoid relegation from Division One. Foxes boss David Halliday took a gamble by handing Len Chalmers his debut and bringing in Ian McNeill for Arthur Rowley. His gamble paid off. McNeill was the hero with the 50th minute goal that secured survival.

SATURDAY 26TH APRIL 1980

Leicester City were on the brink of promotion to Division One after a 2-1 win over Charlton Athletic at Filbert Street. Alan Young and Bobby Smith were on target.

IAIN HUME CELEBRATES HIS OPENER AGAINST SHEFFIELD WEDNESDAY

MONDAY 27TH APRIL 1908

Tommy Shanks got the goal at Stoke City that secured second place in Division Two for Leicester Fosse and a first ever top-flight campaign. Fosse made the trip to the Potteries knowing they needed a point to clinch promotion and Shanks ensured they claimed maximum points with a close-range finish after Fred Shinton's shot had been saved. Horace Bailey, who had recently been capped by England, was in fine form between the posts to deny Stoke a leveller. The team arrived back at Leicester station at 10.25 in the evening and were met by thousands of celebrating fans.

SATURDAY 27TH APRIL 1963

There were 65,000 fans at Hillsborough for the FA Cup semi-final against Liverpool and they saw Mike Stringfellow's 18th minute header send Leicester City through to their third FA Cup final, and second in three years.

TUESDAY 27TH APRIL 1971

Leicester City knew a point at Bristol City would be enough to secure promotion to Division One and they were in no mood to miss their chance. Frank O'Farrell's team dominated from the start at Ashton Gate and Ally Brown grabbed the only goal of the game with three minutes left. Sheffield United's 5-1 win over Cardiff City on the same night clinched the title for City.

SATURDAY 27TH APRIL 1929

Leicester City travelled to Huddersfield Town with hopes of winning Division One for the first time in their history. They were second behind leaders Sheffield Wednesday with two games to play. The Owls led by three points and clinched the title after late drama in both games involving the title challengers. John Duncan put City ahead at Huddersfield and they were denied victory by George Brown's equaliser with nine minutes left following a rare mistake by Foxes goalkeeper Jim McLaren. Sheffield Wednesday grabbed a late leveller against Burnley at Hillsborough and City's chance of championship glory was gone.

SATURDAY 28TH APRIL 1973

Leicester City headed to Anfield aiming to wreck Liverpool's party. The Reds needed only a point to be crowned Division One champions – and Jimmy Bloomfield's battlers made them work for it. The majority of the crowd of 56, 202 breathed a sigh of relief when Mike Stringfellow's goal was ruled out and the Reds got the point they needed from a goalless draw. The Foxes ended the season in 16th place.

SATURDAY 28TH APRIL 2001

Leicester City's 1-0 loss at Newcastle United in the Premier League was a club-record ninth successive defeat. Carl Cort, ironically a target for Foxes boss Peter Taylor the previous summer, got the only goal of the game at St James' Park.

SATURDAY 28TH APRIL 1962

Frank McLintock's goal double ensured Leicester City ended the season with a 2-1 victory over local rivals Nottingham Forest. The result meant that Matt Gillies' team finished 14th in Division One. They fell behind against Forest to Les Julians' first-half opener, but a reshuffled City team with Len Chalmers on the right wing, McLintock at inside-right and Graham Cross leading the line, turned the game after the interval. McLintock netted twice to give Foxes fans plenty to celebrate going into the summer break.

SATURDAY 29TH APRIL 1961

Leicester City handed a debut to 17-year-old Graham Cross and he scored against Birmingham City in a 3-2 win for his home-town club in Division One. Howard Riley and Ken Leek got the other goals for the Foxes. Cross also scored on his debut for City reserves when he was just 15-years-old.

SATURDAY 29TH APRIL 1978

Leicester City's 3-0 win over Newcastle United on the final day of the season came too late to save them from relegation to Division Two. Goals from Mark Goodwin, Roger Davies and Geoff Salmons at least gave Foxes fans an enjoyable end to the season.

SATURDAY 30TH APRIL 1949

Leicester City's first FA Cup final ended in a 3-1 defeat against Wolverhampton Wanderers at Wembley. City were the underdogs – they were battling against relegation from Division Two – and played like it in the first half. Jesse Pye's goals put Wolves 2-0 ahead at the break before Mal Griffiths gave City hope by pulling one back after the goalkeeper spilled Ken Chisholm's shot. The game was decided in the space of a few seconds. Chisholm sparked celebrations among Leicester fans when he found the target from a tight angle on 64 minutes. But the 'goal' was ruled out and within a minute it was 3-1 as Sammy Smyth netted at the other end.

SATURDAY 30TH APRIL 1966

Graham Cross got all the goals in Leicester City's 2-1 win over Nottingham Forest at Filbert Street. His own goal put Forest ahead after 20 minutes. He levelled at the other end a minute later and got the match winner on 33 minutes.

WEDNESDAY 30TH APRIL 1986

Leicester City were left on the brink of relegation to Division Two by a 2-0 defeat against Liverpool at Filbert Street. A crowd of 25,779 saw goals from Ian Rush and Ronnie Whelan send the battle for survival at the bottom into a nerve-wracking final day of the season.

SATURDAY 30TH APRIL 1983

Gordon Milne's Leicester City made it 12 games unbeaten at home with a 0-0 draw against Bolton Wanderers at Filbert Street. City had been expected to beat the side bottom of the Division Two table just seven days after the sensational win at Fulham and the result meant City stayed just outside the top-three promotion places.

MONDAY 30TH APRIL 1962

David Thompson marked his Leicester City debut with a goal against Tottenham Hotspur in the Division One clash at Filbert Street. Graham Cross was the other marksman for City in a 3-2 defeat.

LEICESTER CITY
On This Day

MAY

SATURDAY 1ST MAY 1971

A 2-1 win at Portsmouth capped a 17-match unbeaten run that powered Frank O'Farrell's team to the Second Division championship. John Farrington and Ally Brown were the marksmen.

SATURDAY 1ST MAY 2004

Leicester City drew 2-2 at Charlton Athletic and were relegated from the Premier League. Micky Adams' team went ahead in the fifth minute through a spectacular strike from Marcus Bent before the Addicks hit back through goals from Jonathan Fortune and Paolo Di Canio. Les Ferdinand belted home an unstoppable free-kick with two minutes left, but it wasn't enough to save City from the drop just a year after they had been promoted to the top flight as Championship runners-up.

SATURDAY 1ST MAY 1937

Leicester City clinched the Division Two championship with a 4-1 thumping of Tottenham Hotspur at Filbert Street. Jack Bowers got two goals for City and the others came from Arthur Maw and Tony Carrol.

SATURDAY 2ND MAY 1925

John Duncan's two goals in the 4-0 drubbing of Stockport County at Filbert Street took his tally for the season to 30 and secured the Division Two championship for Leicester City. Arthur Chandler completed an ever-present season with a goal and George Carr added the other. The result completed an astonishing end to the season for Peter Hodge's team. The results from December 6 were as follows: 16 wins, eight draws and only one defeat.

SATURDAY 2ND MAY 1988

Paul Groves became the first Leicester City substitute to score on his debut in the 3-0 win over Huddersfield Town at Filbert Street. Groves, signed by Foxes boss David Pleat from Burton Albion, scored a second-half header after Nicky Cross had earlier netted twice.

SATURDAY 2ND MAY 1981

Jim Melrose got all Leicester City's goals as they ended a relegation season with a 3-2 win at Norwich City that also condemned the Canaries to the drop to Division Two.

SATURDAY 3RD MAY 1980

Larry May headed the only goal at Jimmy Bloomfield-managed Leyton Orient to secure the Division Two title for Jock Wallace's Leicester City team. The result meant the Foxes finished the season with a seven-game unbeaten run that included six wins.

SATURDAY 3RD MAY 1986

Leicester City avoided the drop from Division One on a nail-biting final day of the season thanks to a 2-0 win over Newcastle United at Filbert Street. The result, and a defeat for relegation rivals Ipswich Town at Sheffield Wednesday, meant Gordon Milne's team escaped a relegation that had looked certain for much of a disappointing season. City had lost their previous three games and shipped ten goals before the visit of Newcastle. But the nerves were eased by Ali Mauchlen's first-half strike and Ian Banks netted the second from the penalty spot to prompt celebrations at the final whistle from the majority of a 13,171 crowd.

WEDNESDAY 3RD MAY 2000

Goals from Tony Cottee and Phil Gilchrist clinched a 2-0 win for Martin O'Neill's Leicester City at Liverpool in the Premiership and maintained the Foxes' tremendous record at Anfield. Pegguy Arphexad was the visitors' other hero. The French goalkeeper was in superb form between the posts and Liverpool remembered his performance and ended up signing him.

SATURDAY 3RD MAY 1997

Leicester City and Premier League champions Manchester United battled out a thrilling 2-2 draw in the sunshine at Filbert Street. Steve Walsh and Ian Marshall were the goalscorers for City with Ole Gunnar Solskjaer grabbing both replies for the table toppers.

MONDAY 3RD MAY 1994

Leicester City stayed fourth in Division One with a 1-1 draw against Bolton Wanderers at Filbert Street. Phil Gee got the goal for Brian Little's team in the penultimate game of the regular season before the play-off semi-finals. City had already secured their place in the play-offs.

SUNDAY 4TH MAY 2008

Gary Lineker described this as "the worst day in the club's history". He was right. Leicester City were relegated to the third tier of English football for the first time following a 0-0 draw at Stoke City, who were promoted to the Premier League. Ian Holloway's team made the trip to the Britannia Stadium knowing their superior goal difference would keep them up if they emulated or bettered Southampton's result in their home date with Sheffield United. Southampton fell behind, but went on to snatch a 3-2 win and Leicester could only manage a draw at Stoke.

SATURDAY 4TH MAY 1954

Teenager Bernie Thomas bagged a hat-trick in a 4-0 thrashing of Bolton Wanderers at Filbert Street that came too late to prevent Leicester City finishing bottom of Division One. Thomas became the youngest-ever player to score a hat-trick for the Foxes. He was only 17 years and 350 days old. Derek Hogg scored the other goal.

WEDNESDAY 4TH MAY 1966

Peter Shilton made his debut for Leicester City. He kept a clean sheet in a 3-0 win over Everton at Filbert Street. Jackie Sinclair, Derek Dougan and Paul Matthews got City's goals.

SATURDAY 4TH MAY 1985

Gary Lineker's two goals in a 4-3 defeat at Queens Park Rangers took him to a century of goals for Leicester City in his 214th game. Ian Wilson got the other.

SATURDAY 4TH MAY 1935

Leicester City went into the last game of the season at Portsmouth knowing they needed a victory and Middlesbrough to lose at Chelsea to stay in Division One. City went behind after just six minutes, Gene O'Callaghan levelled, but Middlesbrough's draw at Chelsea meant it wasn't enough.

SATURDAY 4TH MAY 1939

Frank Womack resigned as Leicester City manager before the 2-0 defeat against Wolverhampton Wanderers that was the final game in a season that ended in relegation from Division One.

SATURDAY 5TH MAY 2001

Peter Taylor's Leicester City ended a club-record run of nine successive defeats with a 4-2 thrashing of Tottenham Hotspur at Filbert Street. Gary Rowett, Dean Sturridge, Steve Guppy and Robbie Savage got the goals for City.

MONDAY 6TH MAY 1985

Gary Lineker scored both Leicester City's goals in a 2-0 win over Sunderland in what proved to be his final appearance at Filbert Street.

SATURDAY 6TH MAY 1961

Leicester City were back at Wembley for the FA Cup Final against Tottenham Hotspur. Boss Matt Gillies sprang a surprise before kick-off when he picked Hugh McIlmoyle instead of top scorer Ken Leek and disaster struck when an injury to Len Chalmers meant City had to play with effectively ten men for 70 minutes. Bobby Smith and Terry Dyson got the second-half goals that took the cup back to White Hart Lane.

SATURDAY 7TH MAY 1987

David Pleat's Leicester City denied Middlesbrough promotion to Division One with a shock 2-1 win at Ayresome Park. Middlesbrough knew victory would secure their place in the top flight, but goals from Peter Weir and Gary McAllister secured victory for the visitors and spoiled the party.

SATURDAY 7TH MAY 1949

The end of an era. Septimus Smith, regarded as one of Leicester City's greatest-ever players, made his final appearance for the Foxes. Leicester, beaten in the FA Cup Final by Wolverhampton Wanderers seven days earlier, ended the Division Two season with a 1-1 draw at Cardiff City secured by Jack Lee's goal. In total, Smith played 586 games for the Foxes – including 213 during World War II.

SATURDAY 7TH MAY 1983

Robbie Jones marked his Leicester City debut with a goal in a priceless 2-1 win at Oldham Athletic that took Gordon Milne's team to the brink of promotion to the First Division. Paul Ramsey got the winner for the Foxes to keep them third.

SATURDAY 8TH MAY 1999

A 2-0 win over Newcastle United at Filbert Street lifted Martin O'Neill's Leicester City up to 10th place in the Premiership. Muzzy Izzet and Tony Cottee got the goals for the Foxes.

SUNDAY 8TH MAY 1994

Leicester City's 1-1 draw at Wolverhampton Wanderers ensured they finished the Division One season with a nine-game unbeaten run. Gary Coatsworth got the goal for Brian Little's team that meant they finished fourth in the table and secured a trip to Tranmere Rovers in the first leg of the play-off semi-final.

SUNDAY 9TH MAY 1992

Hide behind the sofa time. Leicester City lost 7-1 at Newcastle United in front of the television cameras. They trailed 6-0 at the break and former Leicester striker David Kelly scored a hat-trick. So did Andy Cole. Fortunately, Brian Little's team had already booked their place in the play-offs. Steve Walsh's goal did give the visiting fans something to cheer. "We drew the second half," he said afterwards.

SATURDAY 9TH MAY 1987

A 0-0 draw at Oxford United meant Bryan Hamilton's Leicester City were relegated from Division One in Alan Smith's last game for the club before he joined Arsenal. At least the draw meant Leicester ended a run of 17 successive defeats away from home. Smith had agreed to join the Gunners two months earlier for an £800,000 fee and was then loaned back to City for the rest of the campaign to help the battle against the drop.

SUNDAY 10TH MAY 1992

Thrashed 5-1 at Cambridge United eight months earlier, Brian Little's team returned to the Abbey Stadium for the Division One play-off semi-final first leg and came away with a 1-1 draw to take into the second leg three days later. Kevin Russell put the Foxes ahead with a sweetly-struck shot from the edge of the penalty area and Leicester-born Dion Dublin levelled for Cambridge.

SATURDAY 11TH MAY 1991

Leicester City avoided what would have been a first ever drop into the third tier of English football thanks to Tony James. The centre-half bagged the goal that beat Oxford United at Filbert Street, sliding in to slam the ball into the roof of the net in front of an ecstatic Kop. Relegation rivals West Bromwich Albion only drew at Bristol Rovers and suffered relegation.

SATURDAY 11TH MAY 2002

It's what the old place would have wanted. Leicester-born Matt Piper grabbed the last ever goal at Filbert Street – and it was a stunner. His diving header secured a 2-1 win over Tottenham Hotspur, but Leicester City still went down from the Premiership with their relegation having already been confirmed. There wasn't a dry eye in the place.

SATURDAY 11TH MAY 1985

Gary Lineker made his last appearance for Leicester City in a 4-0 defeat at Luton Town in Division One. Lineker ended the season with 24 goals and that made him the joint top scorer in Division One with Chelsea striker Kerry Dixon. He went on to join Everton during the summer.

SUNDAY 12TH MAY 1996

Leicester City were held to a goalless draw in the first leg of the semi-final against Stoke City at Filbert Street. Goalkeeper Kevin Poole pulled off an astonishing double save early in the game and Brian Little's team were glad to go into the second leg in the Potteries on level terms.

WEDNESDAY 13TH MAY 1992

Leicester City secured a return to Wembley after 23 years with a 5-0 crushing of Cambridge United in the second leg of the Division One play-off semi-final. The score was tied at 1-1 after the first leg and Tommy Wright (2), Steve Thompson, Kevin Russell and Ian Ormondroyd found the target as Cambridge fell apart.

SATURDAY 14TH MAY 1983

Gordon Milne's team drew 0-0 with Burnley at Filbert Street and that was enough to secure promotion to Division One at Fulham's expense. The result stretched Leicester City's unbeaten run to 15 games. But the promotion celebrations had to wait. The Football League held an enquiry after Fulham complained that their last game at Derby should be replayed because a pitch invasion meant it finished 75 seconds early. The appeal was rejected and Leicester were promoted.

SUNDAY 14TH MAY 1995

A 2-2 draw at Southampton came too late to save City from relegation from the Premiership. They finished the season unbeaten in their last three games, but won only six times throughout the campaign.

SUNDAY 14TH MAY 2000

Leicester City's 4-0 defeat at Sheffield Wednesday on the final day of the season didn't prevent them securing their best-ever finish in the Premier League. Martin O'Neill's team finished the season eighth.

SUNDAY 15TH MAY 1994

Brian Little's team drew 0-0 at Tranmere Rovers in the first leg of the Division One play-off semi-final. Gavin Ward made several crucial saves for Leicester City and Simon Grayson may have used his hand to keep out another goal-bound effort, but the only people that noticed were the crowd and the players.

TUESDAY 15TH MAY 1996

Garry Parker hit a second-half winner at Stoke City to take Leicester City through to the Division One play-off final at Wembley for the fourth time in five seasons.

SATURDAY 15TH MAY 2004

Leicester City bowed out of the Premiership after a 2-1 defeat at Arsenal. The result meant the Gunners ended the season unbeaten, but they had to come from behind to beat Micky Adams' team. Paul Dickov put the Foxes ahead with a 26th minute header following good work from Frank Sinclair. Thierry Henry levelled from the spot and Patrick Vieira grabbed the winner.

SUNDAY 16TH MAY 1993

Redevelopment work on Filbert Street's Main Stand meant the first leg of the Division One play-off semi-final against Portsmouth had to be played at Nottingham Forest's City Ground. Substitute Julian Joachim was Leicester City's second-half goal hero with a stunning solo goal that delighted a Trent End packed with Foxes' fans. He got the ball just inside his own half, sped away from his marker and then accelerated past another couple of challenges before poking home the only goal of the game through the goalkeeper's legs.

MONDAY 16TH MAY 1977

Leicester City were beaten 1-0 at home by Leeds United in Division One in what proved to be Jimmy Bloomfield's final match in charge.

SATURDAY 17TH MAY 1969

Leicester City, beaten in the FA Cup Final by Manchester City three weeks earlier, headed to Manchester United knowing they needed a victory to stay in Division One. The Reds were fired up because it was Sir Matt Busby's last game in charge, but the Foxes got off to the perfect start with David Nish giving them a first-minute lead at Old Trafford. The Foxes were behind by the fourth minute, however, with George Best weaving his magic to put United on level terms before the home side snatched another moments later to take the lead. Rodney Fern grabbed a second for City, but they were beaten 3-2 and suffered the drop to Division Two.

SUNDAY 17TH MAY 1992

Gary Lineker missed the chance to draw level with Bobby Charlton's record haul of 49 goals for England in a 1-1 draw against Brazil in a friendly at Wembley. Leicester City legend Lineker had a first-half penalty saved by goalkeeper Carlos Gallo and David Platt scored four minutes after the break to secure a 1-1 draw for Graham Taylor's team as they prepared for the start of the forthcoming European Championships in Sweden.

TUESDAY 18TH MAY 1994

Leicester City booked their place in the Division One play-off final for a third successive season with a 2-1 win over Tranmere Rovers at a packed Filbert Street. Steve Walsh made an incredible return to the side having been sidelined since the previous September with a cruciate knee ligament injury and set up Ian Ormondroyd's opening goal for City. Tranmere levelled and David Speedie bundled in the second-half winner. Speedie was later sent off along with Rovers keeper Eric Nixon following a clash and missed the final. This proved to be Speedie's final game for Leicester.

SATURDAY 18TH MAY 1974

Leicester City players Peter Shilton, Keith Weller and Frank Worthington were in the England side beaten 2-0 by Scotland at Hampden Park.

TUESDAY 19TH MAY 1993

Brian Little's team booked their return to Wembley for a second successive Division One play-off final by holding Portsmouth to a 2-2 draw at a highly-charged Fratton Park. Leicester City went through 3-2 on aggregate. They trailed at Pompey and then Ian Ormondroyd stabbed home the leveller and Steve Thompson's strike put them ahead. Portsmouth made it 2-2 on the night, but Julian Joachim's first leg cracker proved to be the difference between the sides. On the same night, Chris Pyatt became the first boxer from Leicester to win a world title. He outpointed Sumbu Kalambay for the vacant WBO middleweight championship at the Granby Halls in his home city.

MONDAY 20TH MAY 1940

Leicester City battled to a goalless draw at Birmingham City in the Regional League Midland Division.

WEDNESDAY 20TH MAY 1998

Martin O'Neill's Leicester City drew 0-0 at Tampa Bay Mutiny on their American tour.

WEDNESDAY 22ND MAY 1974

Frank Worthington got his first goal for England in a 1-1 draw against Argentina at Wembley.

MONDAY 23RD MAY 1977

Jimmy Bloomfield resigned as Leicester City manager. The Foxes finished 11th in Division One despite winning only one of their last ten games. That represented a failure to a club who had ambitions of European qualification, at least, going into the season.

FRIDAY 23RD MAY 2008

Ian Holloway was sacked as Leicester City manager. He had failed to prevent the club being relegated to the third tier of English football for the first time in their history.

WEDNESDAY 24TH MAY 1978

Jock Wallace was named Leicester City's new manager. He had previously been in charge at Scottish giants Rangers and inherited a team that had just been relegated to Division Two.

SATURDAY 25TH MAY 1963

Leicester City were beaten 3-1 by Manchester United in the FA Cup Final. City were favourites going into the game. They had been chasing the league and cup double before suffering a slump in form, while United had been battling against the drop. Denis Law and David Herd put United 2-0 ahead before Ken Keyworth's diving header with nine minutes remaining handed Leicester a lifeline. Herd's second goal put the game beyond the Foxes.

FRIDAY 25TH MAY 2007

Martin Allen was appointed Leicester City manager having previously been at MK Dons and Brentford. He didn't last long.

MONDAY 25TH MAY 1992

Leicester City missed out on a place in the newly-formed Premier League after a controversial penalty sent them crashing to defeat in the Division One play-off final at Wembley. The decisive moment in the clash with Blackburn Rovers came in the dying minutes of the first half. David Speedie took a tumble under Steve Walsh's challenge and former Leicester striker Mike Newell stepped up to net from the penalty spot. City were denied a leveller after the break by several goal-line clearances and Muggleton kept out Newell's second spot kick late in the game.

SATURDAY 26TH MAY 1984

Leicester City striker Gary Lineker made his England debut. He came on in the second half of a 1-1 draw against Scotland at Hampden Park. He had ended the previous season with 22 goals in Division One to earn his call-up.

SATURDAY 26TH MAY 1973

Leicester City beat Ipswich Town 3-2 in a pre-season match in Barbados as part of a post-season tournament. Frank Worthington netted twice for the Foxes while Len Glover bagged the other goal.

MONDAY 27TH MAY 1999

The clock was ticking towards a penalty shoot-out in the Division One play-off final at Wembley between Leicester City and Crystal Palace when a free-kick dropped to Steve Claridge just outside the penalty area. He swung a boot at the ball and sent it sailing into the top corner of the net past stunned goalkeeper Nigel Martyn. There was barely time for Palace to restart the game before the referee blew the whistle to herald the end to one of the most dramatic games held at Wembley. Claridge admitted afterwards that he mishit his shot and that the ball went in off his shin. Nobody in Leicester cared. Leicester had earlier fallen behind to Andy Roberts' first-half opener and Garry Parker levelled from the penalty spot with 14 minutes left after Muzzy Izzet had been sent crashing in the box.

WEDNESDAY 27TH MAY 1964

Gordon Banks had one of his less demanding games. He was in goal for England in their 10-0 thumping of the USA in a friendly in New York.

WEDNESDAY 28TH MAY 1969

Leicester City teammates Peter Shilton and David Nish played for England under-23s in the 1-1 draw against their Portugal counterparts in Funchal.

WEDNESDAY 29TH MAY 1996

Leicester City defender Colin Hill was part of the Northern Ireland team that upset the odds by holding Germany to a 1-1 draw in a friendly.

MONDAY 30TH MAY 1994

Leicester City finally won at Wembley and not before time. This was their seventh game at the grand old stadium. Steve Walsh was the Foxes hero in the 2-1 win over Derby County. He had spent most of the previous eight months on the sidelines following a cruciate ligament injury, but came to City's rescue after they fell behind to Tommy Johnson's opener. Walsh levelled with a header from Gary Coatsworth's cross and got the winner with four minutes left. Simon Grayson swung over a cross that Ian Ormondroyd headed goalwards. Rams keeper Martin Taylor got a hand to the ball, but Walsh was there to slot home the winner and send City back into the top flight.

THURSDAY 30TH MAY 1991

Brian Little was appointed Leicester City manager. He succeeded caretaker Gordon Lee, who had saved City from the drop out of the top two divisions for the first time in the club's history just 19 days earlier. Little came with a good reputation having steered Darlington back into the Football League and then taken them to the Fourth Division championship in back-to-back seasons and soon set about lifting spirits at Filbert Street.

MONDAY 31ST MAY 1993

In the space of 12 breathless minutes Leicester City wiped out Swindon Town's 3-0 lead in the Division One play-off final at Wembley to draw level. Julian Joachim belted home the first, Steve Walsh headed home Lee Philpott's cross and Steve Thompson kept his cool to slide home the leveller after Mike Whitlow had made the break and pulled the ball into his path. But with seven minutes left, Swindon striker Steve White went down under Colin Hill's challenge and Paul Bodin netted the penalty to break Leicester hearts at Wembley. Again. That made it six defeats at Wembley for City and followed the previous season's controversial defeat against Blackburn Rovers in the play-off final.

LEICESTER CITY
On This Day

JUNE

THURSDAY 1ST JUNE 2000

Martin O'Neill was announced as Celtic's new manager after four and a half years at Leicester City. In his time at Filbert Street, O'Neill took the Foxes to four successive top-ten finishes in the Premiership – and two League Cups – and will be remembered as one of the best managers in the club's history.

TUESDAY 1ST JUNE 1971

Leicester City started their challenge for the Anglo-Italian Cup with a 1-0 defeat at Cagliari.

MONDAY 2ND JUNE 2003

England played Serbia and Montenegro in a friendly at the Walkers Stadium. Leicester City goalkeeper Ian Walker was named in Sven-Goran Eriksson's squad, but didn't get the chance to play in front of his home crowd. Joe Cole blasted home England's winner after Steven Gerrard had earlier put them ahead and Serbia and Montenegro levelled on the stroke of half-time.

TUESDAY 3RD JUNE 1969

Allan Clarke got two goals for the English FA XI in a 4-0 win over Guadalajara. Clarke's Leicester City teammate Peter Shilton was in goal and he saw the Foxes striker open the scoring with a header before adding another strike.

TUESDAY 4TH JUNE 1971

Jon Sammels netted a goal double and Keith Weller was also on target for Leicester City, but it wasn't enough to prevent a 5-3 defeat against Atalanta in their second game in the Anglo-Italian Cup.

SATURDAY 5TH JUNE 1999

Leicester City defender Matt Elliott was sent off playing for Scotland against the Faroe Islands in a European Championship qualifier. The game ended in a 1-1 draw.

WEDNESDAY 6TH JUNE 1962

Mark Bright, future Leicester City striker, was born in Stoke-on-Trent, Staffordshire.

MONDAY 7TH JUNE 1971

Leicester City grabbed their first win in the Anglo-Italian Cup in their third match with a 2-1 win over Cagliari at Filbert Street. David Nish and Keith Weller were the marksmen.

SATURDAY 7TH JUNE 1947

Leicester City's Division Two season came to a late end with a 2-0 win over Fulham at Filbert Street that was secured by goals from Charlie Adam and Don Revie. The result meant the Foxes finished ninth in Division Two.

SATURDAY 7TH JUNE 1986

John O'Neill became the most capped Leicester City player in the club's history. O'Neill earned his 38th cap for Northern Ireland in the 2-1 World Cup defeat against Spain in Guadalajara. The game took him past Gordon Banks' tally of 37 caps for England.

SATURDAY 8TH JUNE 1940

Goals from Logan and Houghton meant Leicester City finished their Regional League Midlands Division campaign with a 2-0 win over Northampton Town at Filbert Street.

TUESDAY 9TH JUNE 1998

Leicester City goalkeeper Kasey Keller came on as a second-half substitute for the USA in a 4-0 friendly win over FC Gueugnon in France.

THURSDAY 10TH JUNE 1971

Leicester City ended their Anglo-Italian Cup campaign with a 6-0 walloping of Atalanta at Filbert Street. Keith Weller scored twice in the romp and the others came from David Nish, Jon Sammels, Len Glover and John Farrington.

TUESDAY 11TH JUNE 1968

Leicester City completed the signing of Allan Clarke from Fulham for a British record transfer fee of £150,000. Frank Large went to Craven Cottage in exchange. Clarke was an England under-23 international and in two seasons at Fulham had scored 29 and 26 goals, respectively, for the Cottagers to demand the record fee.

MONDAY 12TH JUNE 2000

Peter Taylor became Leicester City boss following Martin O'Neill's departure to Celtic. Taylor had previously been in charge at Gillingham.

FRIDAY 12TH JUNE 1986

Leicester City defender John O'Neill made his 39th and last appearance for Northern Ireland in a 3-0 defeat against Brazil in Guadalajara in the World Cup. He had previously surpassed Gordon Banks' record of international appearances while at Leicester.

SATURDAY 13TH JUNE 1908

Leicester Fosse goalkeeper Horace Bailey earned his fifth and last cap for England in a 4-0 win over Bohemia in Prague. In his five appearances for his country, Bailey conceded only three goals and England netted 35 times at the other end.

SUNDAY 14TH JUNE 1959

Bob Hazell, future City defender, was born in Kingston, Jamaica.

THURSDAY 15TH JUNE 2000

Leicester City midfielder Muzzy Izzet made his debut for Turkey in a 0-0 draw against Sweden in the European Championships.

MONDAY 16TH JUNE 1913

Leicester Fosse set off on a 46-hour, sea and sail journey to Gothenburg for a whirlwind five-match tour paid for by the Swedish FA.

SUNDAY 16TH JUNE 1985

Gary Lineker made his last England appearance as a Leicester City player. He got two goals in a 5-0 win over the USA in a friendly in Los Angeles.

WEDNESDAY 17TH JUNE 1992

Gary Lineker made his final appearance for England. He was substituted after 61 minutes of a vital Euro 92 clash against Sweden in Stockholm. Ironically, he was replaced by former Foxes strike partner Alan Smith. England went on to lose 2-1 and crash out of the tournament with boss Graham Taylor criticised for his decision to withdraw Lineker, who finished with 48 goals from 80 appearances.

GARY LINEKER

WEDNESDAY 18TH JUNE 1913

Leicester Fosse started their five-match pre-season competition in Sweden with a 3-2 win over an Orgryte/IFK Goteburg Combined XI. Fred Mortimer got two goals for Fosse.

THURSDAY 19TH JUNE 1958

Trevor Hebberd, who went on to play for Leicester City, was born in New Alresford in Hampshire.

FRIDAY 20TH JUNE 2008

Nigel Pearson was appointed Leicester City's manager following the dismissal of Ian Holloway. Ironically, Pearson had been in charge the previous season at Southampton, who had stayed in the Championship at City's expense and sent the Foxes crashing out of the top two divisions in English football for the first time in their history.

SATURDAY 21ST JUNE 1913

Fred Mortimer bagged a hat-trick for Leicester Fosse in a 4-0 drubbing of a Stockholm Select XI as part of their five matches in Sweden.

SUNDAY 22ND JUNE 1913

Leicester Fosse made it three straight wins on their tour of Sweden with a 4-2 thumping of the Swedish national team that was inspired by Tommy Benfield's goal double.

WEDNESDAY 23RD JUNE 1971

Jimmy Bloomfield was unveiled as Leicester City's new manager following the departure of Frank O'Farrell to Manchester United. Bloomfield had impressed in taking Leyton Orient to the Third Division championship the previous season.

MONDAY 23RD JUNE 1969

Leicester City striker Allan Clarke was put on the transfer list. City boss Frank O'Farrell said: "Clarke has told me several times that he was not anxious to play in Second Division football. So, it has been decided that it would be in the best interests of the club and player if we put him on the open-to-offers list."

TUESDAY 24TH JUNE 1913

Tommy Benfield netted twice as Leicester Fosse cruised to a crushing 5-1 win over Gefle IF in their pre-season tour of Sweden. Fosse's other marksmen in the victory were Teddy King, Tom Waterall and Fred Mortimer. The result made it four straight wins on the tour with just one game remaining.

TUESDAY 24TH JUNE 1969

Allan Clarke left Leicester City for Leeds United in a £165,000 deal that broke the British transfer record set 12 months earlier when he joined the Foxes from Fulham. In his only season with City, Clarke finished with 16 goals in all competitions. He was man of the match in the FA Cup Final. His 12 goals in the league couldn't keep City in Division One.

TUESDAY 24TH JUNE 1986

Steve Walsh joined Leicester City from Wigan Athletic for a fee of £100,000. He was brought to Filbert Street by boss Bryan Hamilton having helped his Wigan team win the Freight Rover Trophy in 1985.

FRIDAY 25TH JUNE 1971

Neil Lennon was born in Lurgan, Northern Ireland.

WEDNESDAY 26TH JUNE 2002

Leicester City midfielder Muzzy Izzet came on as a second-half substitute for Turkey in the World Cup semi-final against Brazil in Japan. Izzet came on in the 73rd minute for Umit Davala and couldn't help Turkey overhaul the lead given to Brazil by Ronaldo's strike four minutes into the second half. Brazil went on to win the World Cup with a 2-0 victory over Germany in the final. Playing in the semi-final capped a sensational rise for Izzet. He was plucked from Chelsea reserves by then Leicester boss Martin O'Neill in March 1996 and the midfield playmaker went on to become a Foxes legend by helping the team to promotion, four successive Premier League top-ten finishes and two League Cup victories.

WEDNESDAY 26TH JUNE 1968

Future Leicester City striker Iwan Roberts was born in Bangor, Caernarvonshire.

TUESDAY 27TH JUNE 1967

Tony James, future Leicester City defender, was born in Sheffield. He will forever be remembered by Foxes fans for the goal against Oxford United at Filbert Street on the last day of the 1990-1991 season that saved City from what would have been a first-ever relegation to the third tier of English football.

FRIDAY 27TH JUNE 1913

Leicester Fosse ended their five-match Swedish trip in stunning style. They beat the Swedish national team for the second time with a 4-2 win and that made it five straight victories for Fosse on the club's first-ever pre-season tour. Prince Eugene was in the crowd and saw Fred Mortimer bag a hat-trick for Fosse. That took his tally for the historic five-match trip to ten goals. Fosse ended the tour having scored 20 goals and conceded just five at the other end.

FRIDAY 28TH JUNE 1974

Neil Lewis was born in Wolverhampton.

WEDNESDAY 29TH JUNE 1960

Ali Mauchlen was born in Kilwinning, Ayrshire. Mauchlen went on to join Leicester City, along with Motherwell teammate Gary McAllister, in August 1985 and became a hero to Foxes fans.

MONDAY 30TH JUNE 1982

The *Leicester Mercury* reported that Scottish Premier League side Motherwell were hoping to recruit Foxes boss Jock Wallace. Leicester City stated that there had been no contact from Motherwell, but newspaper reports in Scotland suggested a move was imminent. The previous season, Wallace had steered City to the semi-finals of the FA Cup where they were beaten 2-0 by eventual winners Tottenham Hotspur at Villa Park. He also guided the Foxes to the Second Division championship in 1979-1980, although he was unable to keep them in the top flight the following season despite predicting his team could win the title. Wallace had arrived at Filbert Street from Scottish giants Glasgow Rangers in the summer of 1978 and rebuilt the club's fortunes.

LEICESTER CITY
On This Day

JULY

TUESDAY 1ST JULY 1986

Leicester City received a welcome £250,000 windfall when Gary Lineker completed his move to Barcelona from Everton for £2.75m. Lineker had scooped the Golden Boot at the World Cup in Mexico during the summer. He scored six times as England reached the quarter-finals.

TUESDAY 2ND JULY 1985

Goalkeeper Mark Wallington left Leicester City for Derby County for a fee of £25,000. He made 460 appearances for the Foxes – including a club-record 331 consecutive games.

SUNDAY 3RD JULY 1881

Horace Bailey, Leicester Fosse's first England keeper, was born in Derby.

TUESDAY 4TH JULY 2000

Gary Rowett became Peter Taylor's first signing as Leicester City manager when he joined from Birmingham City for £3m. Taylor had taken charge at Filbert Street following Martin O'Neill's decision to join Celtic and was preparing the team for their fifth successive season in the top flight.

TUESDAY 5TH JULY 1898

Pat Carrigan, who went on to be a key member of Leicester City's defence for more than six years, was born in Lanarkshire, Scotland.

TUESDAY 6TH JULY 1971

Former Leicester City striker Hugh McIlmoyle quit football to become a van driver – much to the surprise of Preston North End! He had been on the brink of joining them from Middlesbrough.

FRIDAY 7TH JULY 2000

Callum Davidson joined Leicester City from Premiership rivals Blackburn Rovers for a fee of £1.75m as Foxes boss Peter Taylor continued his summer spending spree.

MONDAY 8TH JULY 1996

Muzzy Izzet completed a £650,000 move from Chelsea to Leicester City. He had been on loan for the last two months of the previous season.

MONDAY 9TH JULY 2001

Leicester City boss Peter Taylor completed the signing of former England goalkeeper Ian Walker from Tottenham Hotspur for a fee of £1.75m. Walker, who had made four appearances for his country at the time, was brought in to compete with Tim Flowers for the goalkeeping jersey in the forthcoming Premiership campaign.

SUNDAY 10TH JULY 1927

Don Revie, future Leicester City player, was born in Middlesbrough.

SUNDAY 11TH JULY 1965

Tony Cottee was born in West Ham, east London. He went on to become one of the success stories of Martin O'Neill's spell as Leicester City manager.

MONDAY 12TH JULY 1982

Jock Wallace resigned as Leicester City manager having led the Foxes into the semi-finals of the FA Cup the previous season. He was strongly linked with a move to Scottish Premier Division side Motherwell and City threatened to take them to court if Wallace joined them following his departure from Filbert Street after four years in charge.

FRIDAY 13TH JULY 1929

Leicester City striker Arthur Chandler got both goals for an FA XI in a 2-1 win over South Africa in Johannesburg.

FRIDAY 14TH JULY 1972

Leicester City announced their intention to abandon their traditional blue and white and wear an all white kit for the forthcoming season.

THURSDAY 15TH JULY 1982

Leicester City fans and board were left fuming as Jock Wallace was unveiled as Motherwell's new manager at a press conference at the Scottish Premier League club.

WEDNESDAY 16TH JULY 1997

Foxes striker Emile Heskey netted twice as Martin O'Neill's Leicester City ran out 7-1 winners at Penzance in a pre-season friendly.

FRIDAY 17TH JULY 1971

Ipswich Town agreed a fee of £100,000 for Arsenal forward Jon Sammels, who had also attracted interest from Leicester City and asked for a few days to think over the offer.

FRIDAY 18TH JULY 1997

Leicester City were 3-1 winners at Torpoint in a friendly. The goals came from Sam McMahon, Steve Guppy and Emile Heskey.

MONDAY 19TH JULY 1982

Alan Smith joined Leicester City from non-league Alvechurch. He was signed by acting boss Ian McFarlane after Jock Wallace's departure to Scottish Premier League side Motherwell.

SATURDAY 20TH JULY 2002

Dennis Wise was sent home from the pre-season tour of Finland and suspended after teammate Callum Davidson suffered a double fracture of his cheekbone following a dispute during a game of cards. The incident led to Wise being sacked by Leicester City.

WEDNESDAY 21ST JULY 1971

Jon Sammels became Jimmy Bloomfield's first signing as Leicester City boss when he joined from Arsenal in a £100,000 deal.

THURSDAY 22ND JULY 1982

Former Coventry City boss Gordon Milne was appointed Leicester City manager following the departure of Jock Wallace to Motherwell.

TUESDAY 23RD JULY 2002

Gary Lineker officially opened the Walkers Stadium as Micky Adams' team prepared for the new season after relegation from the Premier League in the previous campaign under previous boss Dave Bassett.

MONDAY 24TH JULY 1950

Leicester City reported back for pre-season without striker Jack Lee. There had been outrage among fans when news broke that Foxes boss Norman Bullock was selling him to local rivals Derby County for £16,000. Arthur Rowley joined from Fulham as a replacement for Lee.

TUESDAY 25TH JULY 2000

Ade Akinbiyi joined Leicester City from Wolverhampton Wanderers for a club record fee of £5m. Foxes boss Peter Taylor hoped Akinbiyi would fire his team into Europe.

FRIDAY 26TH JULY 1935

Ken Leek was born in Ynysybwl, near Pontypridd in Wales.

THURSDAY 27TH JULY 1989

Wayne Clarke joined Leicester City from Everton more than two decades after brother Allan came to Filbert Street in a record-breaking transfer. As part of the deal, Mike Newell left Leicester for Everton.

FRIDAY 28TH JULY 2000

Darren Eadie was on target as Leicester City won 1-0 against Finn Harps in Ireland.

SATURDAY 29TH JULY 1989

Wayne Clarke bagged his first goals for Leicester City, after joining from Everton, in a 6-1 pre-season win against Swedish side Solleftea. David Puttnam added two and Steve Wilkinson and Paul Groves also scored.

SATURDAY 30TH JULY 1966

Leicester City goalkeeper Gordon Banks was between the posts as England lifted the World Cup at Wembley. England beat West Germany 4-2 with Geoff Hurst scoring a hat-trick. Banks earned his 33rd cap on the greatest day in English football history.

FRIDAY 30TH JULY 1999

Former England goalkeeper Tim Flowers joined Martin O'Neill's team from Blackburn Rovers for a fee of £1.1m. Flowers had helped Blackburn win the Premiership crown in 1994-95 as Jack Walker's millions funded the title charge.

WEDNESDAY 31ST JULY 1946

Allan Clarke, future Leicester City striker, was born in Willenhall, Staffordshire. Clarke's moves to and from Filbert Street two decades later set records for British transfer fees.

LEICESTER CITY
On This Day

AUGUST

FRIDAY 1ST AUGUST 1997

Robbie Savage joined Leicester City from Crewe Alexandra. He was left out of the Railwaymen's team for the previous season's play-offs after refusing to sign a new contract and came to join Martin O'Neill's Premiership team in a deal rising to £650,000.

THURSDAY 1ST AUGUST 1993

David Speedie joined Brian Little's Leicester City from Blackburn Rovers and Foxes fans were divided. Speedie had been a target for City fans since the play-off final in 1992 when he took a tumble under a challenge for Steve Walsh and Mike Newell netted from the penalty spot to end Leicester's Premier League dream.

TUESDAY 1ST AUGUST 1989

Tommy Wright, a cousin of former City favourite Jackie Sinclair, made a £350,000 switch from Oldham Athletic to join David Pleat's team.

FRIDAY 2ND AUGUST 2002

Dennis Wise was sacked by Leicester City after he was found guilty of serious misconduct following an incident on the pre-season tour of Finland that left teammate Callum Davidson with a double fracture of his cheekbone. The dispute followed a game of cards.

SATURDAY 2ND AUGUST 1975

Leicester City started the Anglo-Scottish Cup tournament with a 1-1 draw against Hull City, and without Graham Cross. The club's directors suspended him for continuing to play cricket for Leicestershire in July instead of reporting back for pre-season training. Cross helped Leicestershire win their first ever County Championship trophy in their history, but this incident spelled the beginning of the end for his record-breaking career at Filbert Street that included 599 senior games including appearances in two FA Cup finals and two League Cup finals.

SUNDAY 3RD AUGUST 1997

Martin O'Neill's Leicester City warmed up for their return to the Premiership with a 2-1 win at Northampton Town in a game to mark the Cobblers' centenary. Emile Heskey and Stuart Campbell got the goals for the Foxes at Sixfields Stadium.

SUNDAY 4TH AUGUST 2002

Leicester City's first-ever game at their new Walkers Stadium ground ended in a 1-1 draw with Athletic Bilbao. Tiko put the Spaniards ahead and Jordan Stewart put his name in the history books by bagging the leveller for Micky Adams' team in front of around 24,000 fans.

SATURDAY 5TH AUGUST 2000

Ade Akinbiyi got his first goal in a Leicester City shirt following his club record £5m transfer from Wolverhampton Wanderers. Akinbiyi grabbed City's goal in a 3-1 defeat at Tranmere Rovers in a pre-season friendly.

THURSDAY 6TH AUGUST 1992

David Lowe, a £200,000 signing from Ipswich Town, suffered a shattered cheekbone in the 3-1 pre-season friendly defeat against Borussia Monchengladbach at Filbert Street. Richard Smith grabbed the goal for Brian Little's team against the German visitors.

SATURDAY 7TH AUGUST 1971

Leicester City lifted the Charity Shield at Filbert Street. The match pitted the previous season's Second Division champions against First Division champions Liverpool and Steve Whitworth got the only goal to give Jimmy Bloomfield the perfect start to his spell as Foxes manager. Remarkably, Whitworth never found the target in 400 Football League, FA Cup and League Cup appearances for Leicester.

WEDNESDAY 8TH AUGUST 1984

Leicester City fought out a 2-2 draw with Scottish giants Rangers in a pre-season friendly at Ibrox. John O'Neill and Gary Lineker were on target for the Foxes.

SATURDAY 9TH AUGUST 1997

Robbie Savage made his Leicester City debut as a substitute in a 1-0 win over Aston Villa at Filbert Street on the opening day of the Premier League season. Ian Marshall got the only goal for Martin O'Neill's team.

SATURDAY 10TH AUGUST 1968

Allan Clarke marked his Leicester City debut after his £150,000 British record transfer from Fulham with a goal in the 1-1 draw against Queens Park Rangers. Rangers were making their debut in the top flight after back-to-back promotions and included Clarke's brother Frank in the line-up. Allan put City ahead and Les Allen grabbed an equaliser.

SATURDAY 10TH AUGUST 2002

Brian Deane was the two-goal hero in Leicester City's first league game at the Walkers Stadium, a 2-0 win over Watford in the Championship.

SATURDAY 11TH AUGUST 1979

Alan Young marked his Leicester City debut after a £250,000 transfer from Oldham Athletic with a goal in the 2-1 defeat at home to Rotherham United in the first round of the League Cup.

FRIDAY 12TH AUGUST 1921

Matt Gillies was born in Loganlea, West Lothian.

MONDAY 13TH AUGUST 1984

Leicester City's Centenary Match ended in a 1-1 draw against Aberdeen at Filbert Street. Steve Lynex scored from the penalty spot to ensure honours were even at the end.

SATURDAY 14TH AUGUST 1971

Jon Sammels made his debut for Leicester City in a 2-2 draw against Huddersfield Town. He went on to make 271 appearances for the Foxes. Ally Brown got the opening goal for City with just 45 seconds on the clock and David Nish added Leicester's second goal.

SATURDAY 14TH AUGUST 1993

David Speedie made his Leicester City debut in a 2-1 win over Peterborough United at Filbert Street that was secured by a late goal from Tony James. Steve Thompson grabbed the opener from the penalty spot.

FRIDAY 14TH AUGUST 1998

Frank Sinclair completed a move from Chelsea to Leicester City for a club record fee of £2.55m.

MICKY ADAMS AND BRIAN DEANE

SATURDAY 15TH AUGUST 1987

Leicester City central defender Steve Walsh grabbed the headlines for the wrong reasons after being sent off in the opening-day defeat against Shrewsbury Town at Filbert Street. He was dismissed for breaking the jaw of striker David Geddis, who had earlier grabbed what proved to be the only goal of the game in the Division Two fixture. Walsh was later handed an 11-match suspension by the Football League.

SATURDAY 15TH AUGUST 1998

Martin O'Neill's Leicester City were denied maximum points at Manchester United on the opening day of the Premiership season by David Beckham's last-gasp free-kick. The Foxes opened up a 2-0 lead at Old Trafford through goals from Emile Heskey and Tony Cottee before Teddy Sheringham pulled a goal back to give the Reds hope. The game was in its dying moments when Beckham curled home the goal that broke Leicester's hearts and denied them the perfect start to the campaign. Frank Sinclair made his City debut the day after joining from Premiership rivals Chelsea in a club-record deal.

SATURDAY 16TH AUGUST 1975

An incredible start to the season at Filbert Street. Leicester City and Birmingham City battled out a 3-3 draw in Division One. The Foxes were left with only nine men following the sending-off of Chris Garland, and Jeff Blockley being replaced through injury after City's substitute had been used. City equalised twice to earn a point with Jon Sammels (penalty) and Brian Alderson finding the target for the home side before an own goal by a Blues player secured a draw in front of a crowd of 25,547.

SATURDAY 16TH AUGUST 1980

Jim Melrose made his Leicester City debut in a 1-0 defeat at home to Ipswich Town in Division One. Melrose was brought to Filbert Street by Foxes boss Jock Wallace in a deal worth £250,000 from Scottish Premier League side Partick Thistle.

SATURDAY 17TH AUGUST 1985

Gary Lineker made a swift return to Filbert Street with Everton after joining the Division One champions during the summer in an £800,000 deal. He was upstaged by Mark Bright, whose spectacular double fired Leicester City to a 3-1 win after Bobby Smith had opened the scoring. Russell Osman made his debut for the Foxes after a £240,000 transfer from Ipswich Town.

SATURDAY 17TH AUGUST 1991

Brian Little's first game in charge of Leicester City ended in a goalless draw at Swindon Town in Division Two.

SATURDAY 18TH AUGUST 2001

Peter Taylor's Leicester City suffered humiliation on the opening day of the Premiership season. They were walloped 5-0 at Filbert Street by newly-promoted Bolton Wanderers.

SATURDAY 19TH AUGUST 1950

Arthur Rowley made his Leicester City debut at Bury and his late winner was the first of 265 goals for the club. Rowley went on to become the most prolific scorer in the history of the Football League, but fans were reportedly unhappy when he arrived from Fulham. They felt Rowley was a cheap replacement for popular striker Jack Lee.

SATURDAY 19TH AUGUST 1978

Leicester City boss Jock Wallace handed John O'Neill his debut at Burnley on the opening day of the Division Two season. O'Neill was still a 20-year-old student at Loughborough University at the time, but made an assured debut in a 2-2 draw secured by goals from Billy Hughes (penalty) and Trevor Christie. O'Neill went on to become City's most capped player. He represented Northern Ireland 39 times and appeared in two World Cups.

SATURDAY 19TH AUGUST 2000

Steve Walsh made his 449th and final appearance for Leicester City in the goalless draw against Aston Villa in the Premiership at Filbert Street. The game marked Peter Taylor's first game in charge of the Foxes.

MONDAY 20TH AUGUST 1974

Dennis Rofe was Leicester City's unlikely last-gasp goal hero in a 4-3 win at Birmingham City. He bagged the winner after goals from Frank Worthington (2) and Keith Weller.

SUNDAY 21ST AUGUST 1994

Leicester City made their debut on satellite television and were beaten 3-1 by Newcastle United in front of the Sky Sports cameras. Brian Little's team were making their bow in the Premier League after securing promotion via the play-offs and Julian Joachim grabbed City's goal.

WEDNESDAY 22ND AUGUST 1945

Alan Birchenall was born in East Ham, London.

SATURDAY 23RD AUGUST 1986

Steve Walsh made his debut for Leicester City in the 1-1 draw against Luton Town at Filbert Street after joining from Wigan Athletic. Bobby Smith got the goal for the Foxes in the Division One fixture.

WEDNESDAY 23RD AUGUST 1972

Frank Worthington marked his Leicester City debut with a goal at Old Trafford. George Best got the hosts' reply in a 1-1 draw.

SATURDAY 23RD AUGUST 1980

Division One champions Liverpool were stunned at Filbert Street. Andy Peake lashed home an unstoppable opener from 25 yards and Martin Henderson added a second after the break. Boss Jock Wallace predicted his team would go on to win the Division One title.

SATURDAY 23RD AUGUST 1958

Ken Keyworth made his Leicester City debut in a 2-0 win over Everton at Filbert Street secured by goals from Ken Leek and Howard Riley, watched by a crowd of 34,446.

SATURDAY 23RD AUGUST 1975

A 3-0 defeat at Newcastle United marked the final game of Graham Cross's career with his home-town club. Cross made a club record total of 599 appearances for Leicester City in his 16 years at Filbert Street.

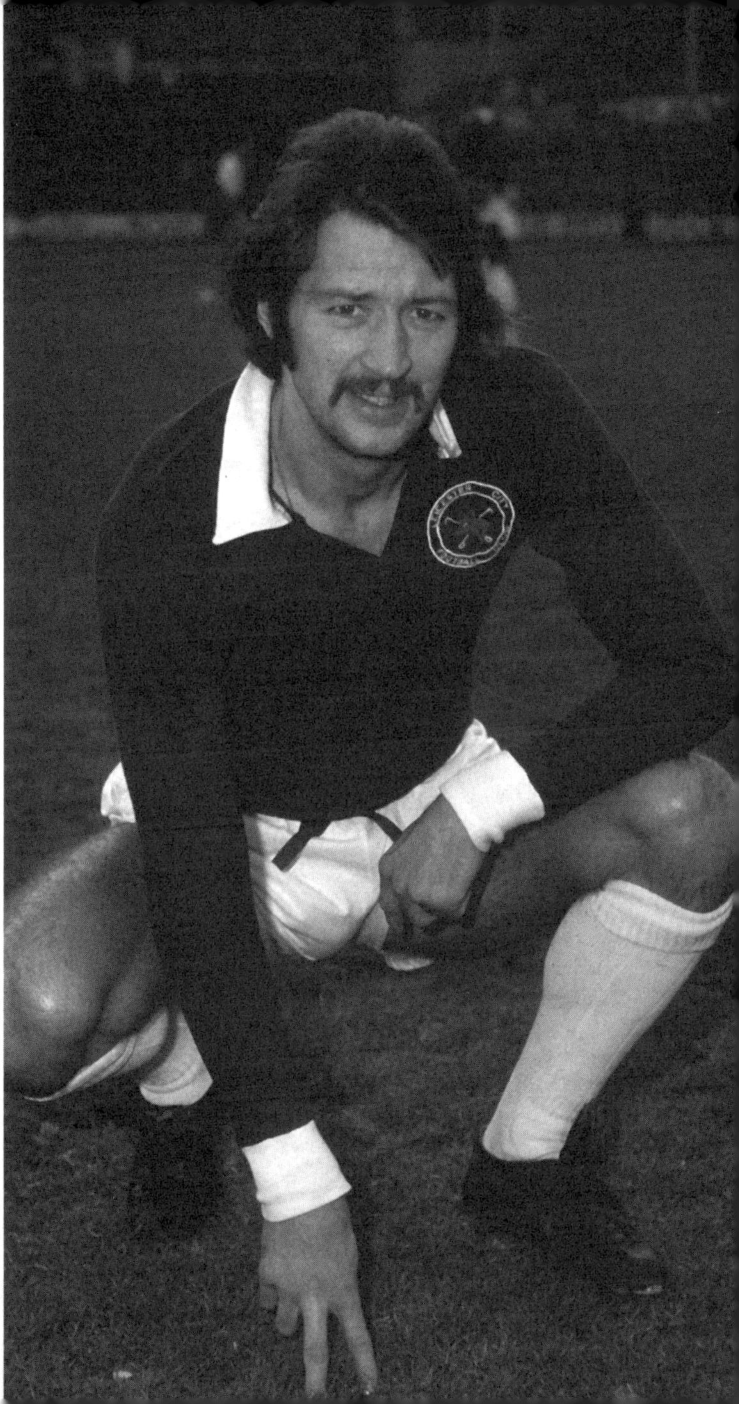
FRANK WORTHINGTON

SATURDAY 24TH AUGUST 1974

Leicester City went into the record books for all the wrong reasons. Mark Wallington – in goal against Liverpool at Anfield because Peter Shilton was in a contract dispute – conceded the quickest-ever penalty. He brought down Steve Heighway after he had intercepted Malcolm Munro's stray pass and Alec Lindsay netted the spot kick. There were just 19 seconds on the clock in the Division One clash. Lindsay netted a second penalty after Keith Weller handled and the Leicester midfielder pulled a goal back for the visitors with 15 minutes left. But the Foxes couldn't conjure up an equaliser.

SATURDAY 24TH AUGUST 1985

Ali Mauchlen made his Leicester City debut as a second-half substitute in a crushing 5-0 defeat at Oxford United in Division One. Mauchlen had arrived earlier in the month from Motherwell, along with Gary McAllister, in a deal worth £250,000.

SATURDAY 25TH AUGUST 1923

Arthur Chandler made his Leicester City debut in a 1-1 draw at Hull City after joining from Queens Park Rangers, where he was a fringe player. He drew a blank at Hull, but didn't have many more. Chandler finished his first season with 24 goals, and his City career with an impressive haul of 273 goals in 419 appearances.

SATURDAY 25TH AUGUST 1990

David Pleat's Leicester City team started the season with a 3-2 win over Bristol Rovers at Filbert Street. David Kelly got the Division Two season off to the perfect start with the opener after just two minutes, Pirates defender Ian Alexander obligingly lobbed into his own net from 30 yards and Tommy Wright almost burst the net with a second-half thunderbolt. They also had two efforts disallowed, but let Rovers back into the game with two goals. The early season optimism didn't last long. The Foxes went on to lose their next seven games and spent the campaign battling against the drop.

SATURDAY 26TH AUGUST 1967

Leicester City snatched an unlikely point at Manchester United after goalkeeper Peter Shilton was injured. Bobby Roberts took over from Shilton between the posts and Mike Stringfellow's goal stunned Old Trafford and secured a 1-1 draw in the Division One clash.

SATURDAY 26TH AUGUST 1933

Arthur Maw was on target after just four minutes on the opening day of the season to set Leicester City on their way to a 3-2 win at Aston Villa. He added another goal and Arthur Lochhead was also on target for the Foxes. On the same day, City's reserve-team striker Jack Gurry was even quicker out of the blocks. He scored just 30 seconds into the second string's game against Charlton Athletic reserves at Filbert Street and went on to get a hat-trick in a 5-1 win that meant the club started with a win double.

WEDNESDAY 27TH AUGUST 1997

Steve Walsh popped up in the sixth minute of injury time to snatch a 3-3 draw against Arsenal at Filbert Street and spark a confrontation with Ian Wright that the Leicester City legend says he's always asked about by City fans. Dennis Bergkamp put the Gunners 2-0 ahead, Emile Heskey pulled one back and Matt Elliott made it 2-2 in the second minute of injury time. Bergkamp put Arsenal back in front a minute later with a stunning goal to complete his hat-trick... then Walsh came to the rescue.

SATURDAY 27TH AUGUST 1988

Goalkeeper Martin Hodge made his Leicester City debut in a 1-1 draw against West Bromwich Albion at Filbert Street. Hodge joined David Pleat's team from Sheffield Wednesday for £200,000 and suffered a stomach muscle injury on his debut that ruled him out for several months. Ali Mauchlen was City's marksman in a game that also marked the City debut of Tony Spearing after his summer move from Norwich City.

TUESDAY 28TH AUGUST 2007

Leicester City's Carling Cup second round tie at Nottingham Forest was abandoned at half-time after City defender Clive Clarke had a suspected heart attack and was rushed to hospital. Leicester were trailing 1-0 at the time.

SATURDAY 28TH AUGUST 1982

Alan Smith made his City debut and Charlton Athletic left Filbert Street with maximum points after a 2-1 win. Bobby Smith got City's goal.

WEDNESDAY 29TH AUGUST 2007

Martin Allen was sacked as Leicester City manager after just four games in charge. He left after a falling out with owner Milan Mandaric. Ironically, his last game in charge was a 4-1 drubbing of Watford that was the best performance of a wretched season that ended in relegation.

SATURDAY 30TH AUGUST 1972

Keith Weller's hat-trick fired Leicester City to a thrilling 3-2 win over Liverpool at Filbert Street. John Toshack grabbed both replies for the Reds. It was 11 years before another player hit a hat-trick against Liverpool with Terry Gibson finding the target three times for Coventry City in Division One.

SATURDAY 31ST AUGUST 1963

Leicester City powered to the top of Division One with a 7-2 demolition of Arsenal at Filbert Street. The goal glut owed much to an injury to Gunners keeper John McClelland. He suffered a fractured collarbone and England striker Joe Baker replaced him between the posts. Leicester led 2-1 when McClelland was injured with Howard Riley's seventh-minute opener being added to by Ken Keyworth. Keyworth added another and David Gibson bagged a brace with the others coming from Mike Stringfellow and Frank McLintock.

SATURDAY 31ST AUGUST 1929

Septimus Smith made his Leicester City debut in a 3-2 defeat at Huddersfield Town and went on to become a Foxes legend. Arthur Chandler got both goals for City at Huddersfield.

LEICESTER CITY
On This Day

SEPTEMBER

SATURDAY 1ST SEPTEMBER 1908

Leicester Fosse's first ever game in Division One ended in a 1-1 draw against Sheffield Wednesday and Jimmy Donnelly had the distinction of scoring their first ever top-flight goal.

SATURDAY 1ST SEPTEMBER 1973

Division One champions Liverpool were held to a 1-1 draw at Filbert Street. Jimmy Bloomfield's Leicester City had started the season with a pair of 1-1 draws away from home and fell behind on 50 minutes. Peter McCormack pulled the ball back and John Toshack powered his header into the City net. Peter Shilton pulled off several fine saves and then the equaliser came on 70 minutes. Alan Birchenall's header from a Len Glover corner flew into the net and City had another point.

SATURDAY 1ST SEPTEMBER 1962

Leicester City stormed to a fourth successive victory that took them up to fourth place in Division One. Bolton Wanderers were the visitors to Filbert Street and they trailed at the break to Jimmy Walsh's goal. The scores were level when Richie Norman put through his own goal, but Matt Gillies' team responded with strikes from Walsh, Graham Cross and David Gibson to claim maximum points. Mike Stringfellow drew a blank having found the target in the opening four games of the season.

SATURDAY 2ND SEPTEMBER 1961

A 5-1 win at Birmingham City lifted Leicester City into the top half of Division One. Ken Keyworth opened the scoring after 11 minutes and the home side fell apart after the break. Gordon Wills pounced twice in as many minutes to open up a 3-0 lead and Jimmy Walsh piled on the misery for the Blues with a brace. Jimmy Bloomfield was on target for Birmingham.

WEDNESDAY 2ND SEPTEMBER 1970

Steve Whitworth made his Leicester City debut in the 4-0 thumping of Bristol City at Filbert Street in Division Two. John Farrington, Bobby Kellard, Ally Brown and David Nish (penalty) scored.

WEDNESDAY 3RD SEPTEMBER 1986

Leicester City grabbed their first win of the Division One season at the third attempt and it proved to be worth the wait. Defending champions Liverpool were toppled 2-1 at Filbert Street in front of a crowd of 16,344 fans. Gary McAllister and Russell Osman got the goals that handed Bryan Hamilton his first win as Foxes manager with the reply coming from Kenny Dalglish.

FRIDAY 4TH SEPTEMBER 1936

Len Chalmers was born in Corby, Northamptonshire.

WEDNESDAY 4TH SEPTEMBER 1957

Derek Hines grabbed his 100th goal for Leicester City in a 3-2 defeat at Sunderland. Tommy McDonald got the other goal for the Foxes.

MONDAY 5TH SEPTEMBER 1927

Leicester City went top of Division One after a 1-1 draw against Sheffield United stretched their unbeaten start to the season to four games. Arthur Chandler got City's goal, but their stay at the top was brief. City were knocked out of the top two days later.

TUESDAY 6TH SEPTEMBER 1994

Leicester City striker Julian Joachim played for England under-21s in a goalless draw against Portugal under-21s at Filbert Street.

SATURDAY 7TH SEPTEMBER 1991

Leicester City's unbeaten start to the Division One season under new manager Brian Little continued with a 2-1 win over Bristol City at Filbert Street that made it five games without defeat. Colin Gibson's unstoppable 25-yard thunderbolt put City on their way to victory and Paul Fitzpatrick bagged what proved to be the winner. The unbeaten start to the season came to an end seven days later with a 3-0 defeat at Middlesbrough.

WEDNESDAY 7TH SEPTEMBER 1960

A 3-2 loss at Wolverhampton Wanderers made it four straight defeats for Leicester City in Division One. Their goals at Molineux came from Jimmy Walsh and Gordon Wills.

TUESDAY 8TH SEPTEMBER 1981

Stewart Hamill got the only goal for Leicester City against Barnsley at Filbert Street – and never played for Jock Wallace's team again. Hamill had been plucked from his job as a Co-Op van driver by Wallace and handed his chance towards the end of the previous season that ended in relegation from Division One. He made a goalscoring start to the 1981-82 season – bagging the only goal against Wrexham at Filbert Street – and followed it three days later with the goal that beat Barnsley to make it three games unbeaten at the start of the campaign. Hamill netted from close range after Jim Melrose's overhead kick had been blocked. But he was replaced by new signing Keith Robson for the next game and never played for Leicester again. Hamill ended up joining Northampton Town and scored after 35 seconds on his debut.

SATURDAY 8TH SEPTEMBER 1973

Leicester City's 2-0 win at Arsenal made it five games unbeaten and left them fourth in Division One. Goalkeeper Peter Shilton kept the scoreline blank at the break with several outstanding saves. Leicester turned on the style after the break and were ahead on 52 minutes. Len Glover gathered Keith Weller's pass, cut inside and rifled a shot just inside the far post and the destiny of the points was settled on 76 minutes when Mike Stringfellow headed home Frank Worthington's cross to double the lead.

SATURDAY 8TH SEPTEMBER 1934

Arthur Chandler hit a hat-trick in Leicester City's 5-0 demolition of Midlands rivals Aston Villa at Filbert Street in Division One to write his name in the record books. He was 39 years and 32 days old when he fired home the treble against Villa, making him the club's oldest-ever scorer of a hat-trick. Tommy Mills and Danny Liddle got the other goals in front of a crowd of 28,548.

WEDNESDAY 9TH SEPTEMBER 1964

Leicester City climbed to fifth in Division One, and just one point behind leaders Chelsea, with a 2-0 win over champions Liverpool at Filbert Street. City had been unbeaten in their opening five games and were soon ahead through Frank McLintock's shot that took a couple of deflections on its way past wrong-footed Reds keeper Tommy Lawrence. It took a couple of good saves from City goalkeeper Gordon Banks to deny Roger Hunt an equaliser and the game was put beyond the visitors with ten minutes left when Ken Keyworth lunged to head home Howard Riley's low cross. There was no way back for the champions.

WEDNESDAY 9TH SEPTEMBER 1959

Gordon Banks made his Leicester City debut in a 1-1 draw against Blackpool at Filbert Street. Banks stepped in to replace the injured Dave McLaren and produced a fine save from Ray Charnley's close-range effort in the first half to keep the scoreline blank at the interval. Ken Leek put City ahead after the break and they were in charge, but Jackie Mudie equalised on the break and Blackpool rattled the woodwork with a late free kick. Banks' teammate Albert Cheesebrough also had reason to celebrate after becoming a father for the second time on the morning of the game.

SATURDAY 10TH SEPTEMBER 1994

A 2-1 defeat at Wimbledon made it five games without a win for Brian Little's Leicester City at the start of their Premier League campaign following promotion via the play-offs. David Lowe got the goal for the Foxes at Selhurst Park. Leicester had claimed their first point of the season in their previous game against Queens Park Rangers.

SUNDAY 10TH SEPTEMBER 1995

Julian Joachim got the winning goal for Leicester City at East Midlands rivals Derby County. The three points took City to the top of Division One. Not a bad day!.

SATURDAY 11TH SEPTEMBER 1982

Steve Lynex and Gary Lineker both hit hat-tricks in a 6-0 demolition of Division Two rivals Carlisle United at Filbert Street. Lynex's treble included two penalties, but he handed the ball to Lineker when the Foxes were awarded a third spot kick later in the game and he fired home.

SATURDAY 11TH SEPTEMBER 1971

Malcolm Munro suffered a broken cheekbone on his Leicester City debut at Ipswich Town. City went on to win the game 2-1 with goals from Jon Sammels and Bobby Kellard securing the points.

SATURDAY 12TH SEPTEMBER 1998

Emile Heskey got Leicester City's goal in a 1-1 draw against Arsenal in the Premiership at Filbert Street.

SATURDAY 13TH SEPTEMBER 1986

Steve Moran made a goalscoring debut in a 2-2 draw at Sheffield Wednesday. A few days earlier he had become the club's record signing when he joined from Southampton in a £300,000 deal.

THURSDAY 13TH SEPTEMBER 2007

Former Nottingham Forest manager Gary Megson was revealed as Leicester City's new boss after the departure of Martin Allen.

WEDNESDAY 13TH SEPTEMBER 1961

Tottenham Hotspur winning the league and FA Cup double meant FA Cup finalists Leicester City were entered in the European Cup Winners' Cup. Their first European campaign started with a 4-1 win at Irish Cup winners Glenavon. City fell behind and hit back through goals from Jimmy Walsh (2), Colin Appleton and Ken Keyworth.

SUNDAY 13TH SEPTEMBER 1992

Russell Hoult was dramatically plucked from the stands, while munching a pre-match hot dog, and handed the keeper's jersey for the home game with Wolverhampton Wanderers, after Carl Muggleton suffered a slipped disc in the pre-match warm-up. It was City's first-ever league fixture to be televised live. 'The Hot Dog Kid' kept a clean sheet and was named Man of the Match after the goalless draw.

GARY MEGSON

THURSDAY 14TH SEPTEMBER 2000

Leicester City embarked on their second Uefa Cup campaign in four seasons with a first round first leg tie against former European champions Red Star Belgrade at Filbert Street. Martin O'Neill's team fell behind in controversial circumstances. The Yugoslav supporters in the East Stand set off flares just before kick-off and the red smoke had not cleared by the time Acimovic belted a 30-yard shot past City goalkeeper Tim Flowers. Leicester were level just before the break when Gerry Taggart headed home and Stan Collymore went close to earning them a lead to take into the second leg.

WEDNESDAY 14TH SEPTEMBER 1999

Leicester City used three goalkeepers in a thrilling 3-3 draw at Crystal Palace in a League Cup second round first leg clash. City were in charge at 3-1 ahead in the second half at Selhurst Park through a first-half own goal and strikes from Neil Lennon and Gerry Taggart. The game turned when goalkeeper Tim Flowers was injured. He had come on to replace Pegguy Arphexad and with all the substitutes used, Theo Zagorakis went between the posts for ten-man City. Palace netted twice in three minutes to draw level, but couldn't force a winner in a frantic last 15 minutes.

MONDAY 15TH SEPTEMBER 1969

Andy Lochhead was the hat-trick hero in a 3-1 win over Bristol City in a League Cup second round second replay at Filbert Street. The Robins were ahead after five minutes, but City got the equaliser eight minutes later when Lochhead fired home and he put Leicester ahead seven minutes after the break. He completed his treble on 59 minutes.

FRIDAY 15TH SEPTEMBER 2000

Steve Walsh ended his spell at Leicester City when he joined Norwich City. Walsh had spent more than 14 years at Filbert Street after arriving from Wigan Athletic and clocked up 449 appearances for the Foxes.

TUESDAY 16TH SEPTEMBER 1997

Leicester City returned to European football after a 36-year absence with a trip to Atletico Madrid in the first round of the Uefa Cup. Ironically, Atletico had ended City's European adventure in their previous campaign, but a repeat didn't look likely when Ian Marshall put Leicester ahead from close range after just 11 minutes at the Vicente Calderon Stadium. They held on to the advantage until late in the game. The introduction of substitute Jose Mari by the home side proved to be decisive. He had a hand in goals from Juninho and Vieri that gave the Spaniards a 2-1 lead to take into the second leg at Filbert Street.

WEDNESDAY 16TH SEPTEMBER 1987

Mike Newell had become Leicester City's record signing when he joined from Luton Town for £350,000 just a few days earlier and he could not have asked for a better start to his career with the Foxes. His diving header on his debut sent Brian Hamilton's team on the way to a 4-1 win over Oldham Athletic at Filbert Street. Finnish striker Jari Rantanen also got his first goal for the club and Gary Ford and Ian Wilson were the other marksmen in the Division Two clash.

SATURDAY 17TH SEPTEMBER 1994

Julian Joachim was the hero as Leicester City claimed their first win of the Premier League season at the sixth attempt. Joachim netted a pair of typically spectacular solo goals in a 3-1 thumping of Tottenham Hotspur at Filbert Street that was captured by BBC television's *Match of the Day* cameras. Ossie Ardiles' Spurs had a star-studded line-up including German international striker Jurgen Klinsmann, who found the target for the visitors. Spurs simply couldn't cope with Joachim's pace, however, and David Lowe bagged City's third goal in front of a 21,300 crowd. City had lost four of their previous five games in the Premier League.

SATURDAY 18TH SEPTEMBER 1926

Leicester City's 4-3 win at Everton took them to the top of Division One for the first time in their history. Arthur Chandler got two goals and the others in a historic game came from Ernie Hine and John Duncan.

TUESDAY 18TH SEPTEMBER 2007

Leicester City travelled to Nottingham Forest for their rearranged Carling Cup second round tie and Gary Megson's team earned plaudits by allowing their local rivals to score straight from the kick-off to ensure the game started as the original fixture ended. They had met three weeks earlier and the game was abandoned at half-time due to Clive Clarke's health problems with Leicester trailing 1-0. To reflect this, Leicester allowed Forest keeper Paul Smith to score unopposed in the first minute. The Foxes equalised and then overturned a 2-1 deficit in dramatic style with two goals in the last two minutes. Richard Stearman grabbed the equaliser and Stephen Clemence curled home a last-gasp free kick to make it 3-2.

SATURDAY 18TH SEPTEMBER 1976

Dennis Rofe launched a free-kick from inside his own half that sailed over the head of Queens Park Rangers goalkeeper Phil Parkes at Filbert Street. Everyone there said it was a fluke, with the exception of Rofe. Chris Garland netted Leicester's other – less spectacular – goal in a 2-2 draw.

SATURDAY 19TH SEPTEMBER 1987

Three days after trouncing Oldham Athletic 4-1, Leicester City beat Plymouth Argyle 4-0 at a rain-lashed Filbert Street. The same four players found the target: Mike Newell, Jari Rantanen, Gary Ford and Ian Wilson.

SUNDAY 20TH SEPTEMBER 1987

Ian Wilson left Leicester City to join Everton for £300,000 after starring in the previous day's drubbing of Plymouth Argyle.

SATURDAY 20TH SEPTEMBER 1930

Ernie Hine's 100th goal for Leicester City was a consolation effort in a 4-1 defeat at Arsenal in Division One. Hine reached the landmark in his 185th game for the club.

PAUL SMITH CELEBRATES HIS FIRST MINUTE OPENER

TUESDAY 21ST SEPTEMBER 1993

Rochdale were hit for six in a League Cup second round first leg tie at Spotland. The travelling Leicester City fans must have feared the worst when Brian Carey's own goal put 'Dale ahead after just five minutes. Mike Whitlow levelled and the Foxes hammered in five more goals in the second half. Steve Walsh, Steve Thompson, David Oldfield, David Speedie and Ian Ormondroyd were the marksmen for Brian Little's side in the romp.

SATURDAY 21ST SEPTEMBER 1985

Tony Sealy scored on his Leicester debut in the 2-1 defeat at Birmingham City after joining the Foxes from Fulham. He didn't get many more.

SUNDAY 22ND SEPTEMBER 1996

Martin O'Neill's team announced their arrival as a Premiership force with a 2-1 win at Tottenham Hotspur. Leicester City started better and it was no surprise when Steve Claridge slid in at the far post to put them ahead after 22 minutes. He was injured while scoring and was replaced by Ian Marshall, who proved to be Leicester's match-winner at White Hart Lane after Clive Wilson had netted a 64th minute leveller for the home side. Marshall headed home the winner for the visitors with four minutes left.

FRIDAY 23RD SEPTEMBER 1938

David Gibson was born in Winchburgh, West Lothian and went on to become a Leicester City legend.

SATURDAY 24TH SEPTEMBER 1977

Frank Worthington made his last appearance for Leicester City in the 3-0 defeat at home to Nottingham Forest. Worthington headed to Bolton Wanderers and the following season was Division One's top goalscorer with 24 goals.

SATURDAY 24TH SEPTEMBER 1938

Mal Griffiths made his Leicester City debut in a goalless draw against Bolton Wanderers at Filbert Street. He joined City from Arsenal for a bargain £750 seven months after marking his Gunners debut with a goal against Leicester. Griffiths went on to help Arsenal win Division One before joining City.

SATURDAY 25TH SEPTEMBER 1926

Leicester City stayed top of Division One after a 4-0 thrashing of Blackburn Rovers at Filbert Street. The goals came from Arthur Lochhead, Ernie Hine, John Duncan and Arthur Chandler.

FRIDAY 26TH SEPTEMBER 1947

David Nish was born in Burton-upon-Trent.

SATURDAY 27TH SEPTEMBER 1997

Ian Marshall and Graham Fenton got the goals in a 2-0 win at Barnsley that lifted Leicester City up to third in the Premiership and secured the Manager of the Month award for Foxes boss Martin O'Neill.

WEDNESDAY 27TH SEPTEMBER 1961

Goals from Gordon Wills, Ken Keyworth and Hugh McIlmoyle secured a 3-1 win for Leicester City over Glenavon in the second leg of their European Cup Winners' Cup first round tie. That completed a 7-2 aggregate win and set up a clash against Atletico Madrid.

THURSDAY 28TH SEPTEMBER 2000

Leicester City's Uefa Cup first round, second leg tie at Red Star Belgrade was switched to Vienna because of unrest in the Serbian capital. They went into the game level at 1-1 after the first leg, but fell behind early on. Muzzy Izzet forced the ball home from close range to level the scores just before half-time, but Red Star stepped up a gear after the break and netted twice more to make it 3-1 on the night and 4-2 on aggregate.

WEDNESDAY 28TH SEPTEMBER 1988

Leicester City stormed to a 4-1 win over Division Two leaders Watford in a League Cup second round, first leg tie at Filbert Street. Paul Reid put City ahead, Watford levelled and Steve Walsh put the Foxes in front at the break. Nicky Cross and Gary McAllister bagged a quick-fire second-half double to ease City into a comfortable lead going into the second leg.

SATURDAY 28TH SEPTEMBER 1985

Gary McAllister made his debut in a 1-0 win over Ipswich Town at Filbert Street that was secured by Alan Smith's strike.

SATURDAY 29TH SEPTEMBER 1990

David Pleat's side suffered a seventh straight defeat at Middlesbrough. They were thumped 6-0 at Ayresome Park and Steve Walsh was sent off. Leicester trailed 1-0 six minutes before the break when Walsh was sent off for a professional foul and Middlesbrough twisted the knife. They found the target three more times before the interval and completed the rout after the break. The loss equalled Leicester's record losing run in the league.

SUNDAY 30TH SEPTEMBER 2001

Peter Taylor was sacked as Leicester City manager. The previous day, City had lost 2-0 at Charlton and that meant they had taken only one point from their opening eight games in the Premiership. Junior Lewis was sent off at Charlton Athletic.

TUESDAY 30TH SEPTEMBER 1997

Leicester City bowed out of the Uefa Cup after a 2-0 defeat against Atletico Madrid in the second leg of their first round clash. That meant the Spaniards went through 4-1 on aggregate, but Leicester made them battle and the outcome could have been different. The referee waved away four penalty appeals with Muzzy Izzet being aggrieved after being sent crashing three times. City were handed a lift when Lopez was sent off, but the Foxes were also left with only ten men after Garry Parker was dismissed. Parker and the crowd were stunned when he was punished for taking a free-kick too quickly. Juninho and Kiko bagged breakaway goals to send Madrid through.

SATURDAY 30TH SEPTEMBER 1995

Emile Heskey's first goal for Leicester City secured a 1-0 win at Norwich City and kept them on top of Division One. Heskey came off the bench for only his third appearance for the Foxes and turned home David Lowe's cross with only three minutes remaining. City boss McGhee handed a debut to defender Franck Rolling and the Canaries line-up included future Leicester players Darren Eadie and Ade Akinbiyi.

LEICESTER CITY
On This Day

OCTOBER

SATURDAY 1ST OCTOBER 1938

Leicester City were on the receiving end of an 8-2 hammering at Leeds United. They suffered an early setback with the loss of goalkeeper Sandy McLaren through injury and the presence of Fred Sharman and then Billy Frame between the posts couldn't prevent the home side's rout.

SUNDAY 1ST OCTOBER 2000

Leicester City ended the day at the summit of the top flight of English football for the first time since August 1963. The 0-0 draw at Sunderland and Thierry Henry's spectacular winner against Manchester United meant Peter Taylor's team were on top of the Premier League. The result stretched their unbeaten start to the season to eight games and goalkeeper Tim Flowers was in fine form. He conceded only two goals in open play during that spell and was named the Carling Premiership Player of the Month.

SATURDAY 2ND OCTOBER 1926

Leicester City's two-week stay at the top of Division One came to an end after a 5-3 defeat at Huddersfield Town. Jack Bamber got two goals for City and Arthur Chandler the other in the defeat.

SATURDAY 2ND OCTOBER 2004

Preston North End goalkeeper Andy Lonergan scored against Leicester City in a 1-1 draw at the Walkers Stadium.

SATURDAY 2ND OCTOBER 1954

A crowd of 42,486 – the highest attendance for a league game at Filbert Street – watched Leicester City and Arsenal battle out a 3-3 draw in Division One. Arthur Rowley netted twice – once from the penalty spot – and Derek Hines got the other in a six-goal thriller.

SATURDAY 3RD OCTOBER 1992

Julian Joachim made his Leicester City debut in a 2-1 win over Barnsley at Filbert Street. Simon Grayson and Bobby Davison got the goals for Brian Little's team.

SATURDAY 4TH OCTOBER 1975

A goalless draw at Manchester United's Old Trafford ended a run of three straight defeats for Leicester City. The result left City looking for their first win of the season after 11 games of the Division One campaign.

WEDNESDAY 5TH OCTOBER 1977

Frank McLintock's Leicester City ended a run of five straight defeats in Division One by battling to a goalless draw at Chelsea. Tommy Williams made his debut for the Foxes at Stamford Bridge.

WEDNESDAY 5TH OCTOBER 1994

Leicester City were in trouble at the bottom of the Premiership and Brighton & Hove Albion piled on the misery for Brian Little's team. The visitors from the Second Division won 2-0 to complete a 3-0 win in the second round of the League Cup. It was City's first defeat against a team from a lower division since Lincoln City triumphed over two legs in 1982. Brighton led going into the second leg through a controversial late goal in the first meeting between the sides and Stuart Munday stunned the home crowd by making it 2-0 on aggregate after just 16 minutes. David Oldfield stepped off the bench to make his first appearance of the season, but couldn't inspire City and Kurt Nogan completed the humiliation with a second goal for the Seagulls with just six minutes remaining.

SATURDAY 6TH OCTOBER 1962

Matt Gillies took his Leicester City team to Division One champions Ipswich Town, while placed fifth in the table. But they had been the victims of a League Cup giant-killing at Charlton Athletic in the previous game and were without playmaker David Gibson through injury. Gillies reshuffled his team with Frank McLintock taking over the inside-left position and Graham Cross stepping in at wing-half. It worked. Cross had a starring role in the match at Portman Road that was won by McLintock's second-half goal.

SATURDAY 7TH OCTOBER 1967

Mike Stringfellow was the goal hero as struggling Leicester City turned the formbook on its head to topple Division One leaders Liverpool at Filbert Street. Three successive defeats had left Matt Gillies' team bottom of the table and it was no surprise when Ian St John struck in the 27th minute to give the Reds the advantage at half-time. City, with full-back Willie Bell making his home debut, hit back after the break. Stringfellow netted twice and goalkeeper Peter Shilton marked his return to the side following an injury with several crucial saves to deny the visitors an equaliser in an exciting climax.

SATURDAY 8TH OCTOBER 1988

Jimmy Quinn rifled home an unstoppable free-kick from 20 yards to clinch a 1-0 win for David Pleat's Leicester City against Brighton & Hove Albion in Division Two. It was only the Foxes' third win in their opening ten games of the season.

SATURDAY 9TH OCTOBER 1926

Arthur Chandler reached the landmark of 100 goals for Leicester City with a double strike in the 2-1 win over Sunderland at Filbert Street. It was his 140th game for the Foxes.

SATURDAY 10TH OCTOBER 1992

Bobby Davison and Julian Joachim were on target in a 2-0 win at Birmingham City that secured a third straight win for Brian Little's Leicester City and lifted them up to fourth in the Division One table.

SATURDAY 10TH OCTOBER 1982

Leicester City's 3-0 win at Bolton Wanderers took them back into the top ten in Division Two. Jim Melrose was the two-goal hero and Alan Young was also on target for the Foxes.

MONDAY 11TH OCTOBER 2004

Leicester City announced they had accepted Micky Adams' resignation as manager. The Foxes were 12th in the Championship at the time and Adams was under pressure from supporters. He had failed to keep City in the Premier League the previous season.

WEDNESDAY 12TH OCTOBER 1960

Leicester City played their first game in the League Cup and there were just 7,070 fans at Filbert Street to see Jimmy Walsh write his name in the record books. Walsh became the first player to score a hat-trick in the competition's history with a treble in a 4-0 demolition of Fourth Division Mansfield Town. Albert Cheesebrough got the other goal and the game marked the only senior appearance in a City shirt for youth team goalkeeper Rodney Slack. The League Cup was introduced to take advantage of the widespread installation of floodlights around the country and to introduce a sudden-death element to the first half of the season when the divisions are still taking shape. Only 87 clubs entered the first League Cup.

SATURDAY 13TH OCTOBER 1973

In a game well remembered by Leicester City fans and Alan Birchenall, the Foxes came close to becoming the first team to halt Leeds United. The sides shared four goals in a breathless first half. City were 2-0 ahead inside the opening 20 minutes. Frank Worthington bagged the opener and Birchenall slammed home a 30-yard volley. Leeds hit back and were level before the break through Mick Jones and Billy Bremner. Don Revie went on to lead Leeds to the First Division title with a record points haul.

TUESDAY 13TH OCTOBER 1964

Mike Stringfellow's goal secured a third successive victory for Leicester City at Anfield. Nine minutes after the break, Billy Hodgson sent over a low cross and Stringfellow rammed the ball into the roof of the net to continue Leicester's jinx over the Reds.

SATURDAY 13TH OCTOBER 1894

Leicester Fosse crushed Notts Olympic in an FA Cup qualifying-round clash. David Skea grabbed a hat-trick for Fosse and there were four apiece for both 'Tout' Miller and Willie McArthur. Johnny Hill rounded up the haul with a double – 13-0!

SATURDAY 14TH OCTOBER 2000

Leicester City's longest ever spell at the top of the top flight of English football came to an end after 13 days. They were beaten 3-0 by Manchester United at Filbert Street and knocked off their Premier League perch. Teddy Sheringham scored twice for the visitors and Ole Gunnar Solskjaer bagged the other.

TUESDAY 14TH OCTOBER 1997

Leicester City skipper Steve Walsh and teammate Julian Watts both spent the night in hospital after the League Cup holders crashed out after defeat at Grimsby Town. Martin O'Neill's team were without six first-team regulars for the third round clash, but were on course for victory when Ian Marshall headed home a Robbie Savage cross after 16 minutes. Former Leicester player Kevin Jobling drew the home side level in the 68th minute and then came the game's turning point. Goalkeeper Kasey Keller raced from his goal, punched Watts rather than the ball and Mariners striker Steve Livingstone accepted the gift. Walsh collided with a post when he tried to clear the ball and joined Watts in the local hospital. Livingstone added another five minutes later to make it 3-1.

SATURDAY 14TH OCTOBER 1967

Mike Stringfellow grabbed a goal double in a 5-1 win at Southampton – but it was Leicester City goalkeeper Peter Shilton who grabbed the headlines. Shilton punted the ball forward from the edge of his area and with the help of a strong wind and the hard surface, watched it bounce over Saints goalkeeper Campbell Forsyth and into the net. That put the seal on City's first-ever win at The Dell and meant Shilton emulated Pat Jennings after the Arsenal goalkeeper netted in the Charity Shield two months earlier. The match was also memorable for Leicester-born striker Alan Tewley, who marked his first start in the senior side with a goal. Jackie Sinclair was City's other marksman.

SATURDAY 15TH OCTOBER 1983

Leicester City's match against Southampton was abandoned after 22 minutes because of a waterlogged pitch. BBC Television's *Match of the Day* cameras were there to capture City winger Steve Lynex doing his breaststroke in one of the many puddles on the pitch before the referee decided the conditions were too bad.

SATURDAY 16TH OCTOBER 1999

Steve Guppy and Tony Cottee got the goals for Leicester City in a 2-1 win over Southampton at Filbert Street. The result lifted the Foxes up to fifth place in the Premiership table.

SATURDAY 16TH OCTOBER 1993

There was late drama in Leicester City's clash at Charlton Athletic. Steve Agnew appeared to have secured a point for City with a late goal, but the Addicks were awarded a controversial penalty in the dying moments and Darren Pitcher smashed the spot kick past Gavin Ward to break Leicester's hearts.

SATURDAY 17TH OCTOBER 1964

Leicester City made their first appearance on BBC Television's *Match of the Day* – and the viewers were thrilled by a 3-2 win over Nottingham Forest at Filbert Street. Billy Hodgson headed Leicester in front after the goalkeeper could not reach a corner, but Forest came back. Colin Addison smacked a shot against the crossbar and Gordon Banks pulled off several fine saves before Forest drew level. City were back in front just 60 seconds later. Bobby Svarc was bundled over in the box and Colin Appleton stepped up to convert the penalty. Forest were level again through a deflected shot, but Leicester snatched maximum points with five minutes left. Appleton swung over a free-kick from the left and Mike Stringfellow got above the defence to steer his header into the bottom corner to leave City eighth in the Division One table.

SUNDAY 18TH OCTOBER 1970

Gerry Taggart was born in Belfast.

MONDAY 19TH OCTOBER 1998

An emotional night at Filbert Street as Leicester City fans implored boss Martin O'Neill to stay during the 2-1 win over Tottenham Hotspur. Fans held posters pleading: "Don't Go Martin!" after Leeds United made public their interest in City's manager. Ironically, the manager's post at Elland Road had been left vacant by George Graham's decision to resign and take over at Tottenham. Graham brought his new team to Leicester and the game went according to the script with Muzzy Izzet belting home a spectacular late winner to secure a 2-1 win for the Foxes. Les Ferdinand, who went on to play for Leicester, had earlier put the visitors ahead. Emile Heskey levelled and Izzet won the game by crashing home an unstoppable volley after a clearance dropped to him.

SATURDAY 20TH OCTOBER 1928

Leicester City's 10-0 win over Portsmouth at Filbert Street remains the biggest league win in the club's history – and is also remembered for Arthur Chandler and the six swans! The meeting between the sides in Leicester eight months earlier had ended in a 6-2 win for the Foxes and they were on course to better that after romping into a 5-0 half-time lead. Chandler's fifth goal made it 7-0 in the 71st minute and legend has it that a flock of five swans flew over the ground – one for each of his goals. A few minutes later, after Ernie Hine had bagged number eight, a sixth swan is said to have appeared as if imploring Chandler to add another goal. He did just that and Hine completed the scoring with his hat-trick strike.

SATURDAY 20TH OCTOBER 1984

Mark Wallington made his 460th and last appearance for Leicester City in a 5-0 defeat at Sheffield Wednesday. Imre Varadi put three goals past Wallington and he went on to join Derby County at the end of the season.

SATURDAY 21ST OCTOBER 1989

David Pleat's team went into the home date with Swindon Town in deep trouble at the bottom of Division Two. The opening 12 games had brought only one win and a crippling injury list meant 23 players had already been used. Paul Reid proved to be City's match-winner with a pair of stunning strikes. A left-footed player, Reid was often used on the right side of midfield and his ability to cut inside and shoot from range proved to be the difference between the sides. He put City ahead eight minutes after the restart from 30 yards and after Ossie Ardiles' team levelled, Reid blasted home another long-range effort on 66 minutes to secure three precious points.

SATURDAY 22ND OCTOBER 1961

Jack Lorrie and Albert Cheesebrough got the Leicester City goals in a 2-2 draw against West Bromwich Albion in Division One at Filbert Street.

SATURDAY 23RD OCTOBER 1976

Keith Weller was on target twice as Leicester City dished out a 4-1 thrashing to Arsenal at Filbert Street. The other goals came from Steve Earle and a Frank Worthington penalty.

SATURDAY 23RD OCTOBER 1982

Gary Lineker bagged a hat-trick in a 4-0 win at Derby County that kept Gordon Milne's Leicester City in touch with the Division Two pacesetters. He completed his hat-trick with a last-minute header and strike partner Alan Smith got the other.

WEDNESDAY 23RD OCTOBER 1957

Leicester City marked the installation of floodlights at Filbert Street with a friendly against Borussia Dortmund. Willie Gardiner grabbed City's goal in a 1-0 win.

WEDNESDAY 24TH OCTOBER 2007

Gary Megson resigned as Leicester City manager to take over at Premier League strugglers Bolton Wanderers. He was at the Walkers Stadium for just 41 days and was in charge for nine league games. The night before he resigned, Leicester lost 1-0 at home to Sheffield United.

WEDNESDAY 25TH OCTOBER 1961

Leicester City's Uefa Cup second round first leg against Atletico Madrid ended in a 1-1 draw at Filbert Street. Mendoza got a last-gasp leveller for the Spaniards after Ken Keyworth had put City ahead. Keyworth had another goal ruled out.

WEDNESDAY 26TH OCTOBER 1988

Another stunning fightback against Swindon Town at Filbert Street. The previous season, Leicester City overturned a 2-0 deficit with eight minutes left to win a five-goal thriller and there was more drama when the sides clashed again. The visitors swept into a 3-0 lead inside the opening 28 minutes. Gary McAllister gave the home fans hope with a 64th minute penalty and within 11 minutes, the scores were level. Phil King's own goal made it 3-2 and McAllister bagged the equaliser. City went close to finding a winner in a frantic climax.

WEDNESDAY 26TH OCTOBER 1983

Leicester City's 3-0 win over Arsenal at Filbert Street proved to be the season's turning point. Following the previous campaign's promotion, Gordon Milne's team had struggled to adapt to the top flight and went into the clash against Arsenal one place above the bottom having claimed just one win in their opening 14 games. Bob Hazell made his return for Leicester at the back and it was his presence at the other end of the pitch that helped create the opening for Gary Lineker to fire City in front. Steve Lynex doubled the lead before the break and Alan Smith completed the scoring in the last minute. The Foxes went on to climb the table to safety.

SATURDAY 26TH OCTOBER 1991

Steve Thompson made the perfect start to his Leicester City career after making the move from Luton Town. He stepped off the bench at Oxford United to net a stylish winner from the edge of the penalty area. Tommy Wright had bagged City's opener with a dipping volley.

SATURDAY 27TH OCTOBER 1984

Gary Lineker bagged a hat-trick against Aston Villa in just 29 minutes in the first half to send Leicester City on their way to a crushing 5-0 win. Steve Lynex (penalty) and Peter Eastoe were the other marksmen for the Foxes.

WEDNESDAY 28TH OCTOBER 1981

It was six years since Leicester City had won a tie in the League Cup and that miserable run came to an end at Filbert Street. City trailed 1-0 from the second round, first leg at Third Division Preston North End, but avoided an embarrassing exit with a four-goal blitz. Keith Robson levelled the scores on aggregate after 28 minutes with what proved to be his only goal for Leicester; Steve Lynex put them ahead ten minutes later. Early in the second half, an own goal put City further clear and Jim Melrose slammed home a late fourth from close range.

FRIDAY 28TH OCTOBER 1960

John Sjoberg made his Leicester City debut in a 2-1 defeat at Cardiff City. Jimmy Walsh got Leicester's goal and Sjoberg went on to make a total of 413 appearances for the Foxes.

SATURDAY 28TH OCTOBER 2000

Arnar Gunnlaugsson stepped off the bench to get Leicester City's winner against Derby County in the Premiership. Muzzy Izzet got the other goal in a 2-1 win.

SATURDAY 29TH OCTOBER 1983

Leicester City secured their first win of the Division One season at the 11th attempt. Alan Smith and Paul Ramsey got the goals for Gordon Milne's team in a 2-0 win over Everton at Filbert Street.

SATURDAY 30TH OCTOBER 1999

Leicester City climbed to fifth in the Premiership with a 3-0 victory over Sheffield Wednesday at Filbert Street. Gerry Taggart was the hero with two goals and Tony Cottee grabbed the other for Martin O'Neill's side.

THURSDAY 31ST OCTOBER 1974

Muzzy Izzet was born in Mile End, London.

LEICESTER CITY
On This Day

NOVEMBER

SATURDAY 1ST NOVEMBER 1884

History was made on this day. Leicester Fosse played their first-ever competitive match. It wasn't very competitive, though. They thumped Syston Fosse 5-0 at a venue just off Fosse Road with West and Milton Johnson getting two goals each, with Dingley grabbing the other, to get the club off to a winning start.

MONDAY 1ST NOVEMBER 2004

It was announced that Craig Levein was Leicester City's new manager. He quit Scottish Premier League side Heart of Midlothian to take the job. He replaced Micky Adams after his resignation.

WEDNESDAY 2ND NOVEMBER 1988

Leicester City, mid table in Division Two under David Pleat, dumped Division One leaders Norwich City out of the League Cup in a third round tie at Filbert Street. Mike Newell put Leicester ahead in the first half and Paul Reid rifled home a late clincher in front of the Kop after Ali Mauchlen's fearless challenge on the edge of the box had sent the ball into his path.

SATURDAY 2ND NOVEMBER 1963

Leicester City had been Liverpool's bogey team the previous season with victory in the FA Cup semi-final, and a win double in Division One, and pulled off another win at Anfield. Ken Keyworth, the scorer of the opening goal in the win on Merseyside the previous campaign, gave Matt Gillies' team a first-half lead. Liverpool swept forward in pursuit of an equaliser and found City goalkeeper Gordon Banks in his best form. His saves brought applause from the Kop.

SATURDAY 2ND NOVEMBER 1968

Andy Lochhead made his Leicester City debut in a goalless draw at Newcastle United.

SATURDAY 3RD NOVEMBER 1980

Leicester City climbed three places up to third in the Division Two table with a 3-1 win at Watford that was secured by two goals from Bobby Smith – including a penalty – and another from Andy Peake.

SATURDAY 4TH NOVEMBER 1972

George Best was on target at Filbert Street as Leicester City and Manchester United shared four goals in Division One. Jimmy Bloomfield's Foxes went into the game struggling for form. They were 20th in the table, two places above their visitors. Best fired United ahead from an acute angle after 15 minutes and Leicester were level five minutes before the break when Jon Sammels netted. Wyn Davies restored United's advantage on the hour, but John Farrington hauled Leicester level eight minutes later.

THURSDAY 4TH NOVEMBER 1920

Jack Lee was born in Sileby.

SUNDAY 5TH NOVEMBER 1995

Leicester City boss Mark McGhee handed debuts to goalkeeper Zeljko 'Spider' Kalac and Pontus Kaamark at West Bromwich Albion. Kalac was finally granted his work permit having joined from Sydney United in the summer and Sweden international Kaamark arrived from IFK Goteborg for £840,000. McGhee's team were never better than they were at the Hawthorns in the first half. Scott Taylor (two) and Iwan Roberts put them in charge at 3-0 ahead before Kalac blundered to let the Baggies get it back to 3-2.

SATURDAY 6TH NOVEMBER 1993

A 3-0 win over Southend United at Filbert Street sent Leicester City to the top of Division One. The goals came from Julian Joachim, David Oldfield and a Steve Thompson spot kick.

SATURDAY 7TH NOVEMBER 1987

Mark Venus, a target for Leicester City's boo-boys for the past few months, was the hero of a dramatic 3-2 win over Swindon Town at Filbert Street in Division Two. Future Foxes striker Jimmy Quinn bagged Swindon's second as the visitors took a 2-0 lead and City clawed their way back. Paul Ramsey and Steve Walsh were on target to draw the sides level and Venus thumped home an unstoppable 25-yarder in the dying seconds to snatch victory and earn the acclaim of the City supporters.

WEDNESDAY 8TH NOVEMBER 1995

Leicester City goalkeeper Zeljko 'Spider' Kalac ended the League Cup third round replay against Bolton Wanderers with his head in his hands after his blunders gifted the Premier League visitors a 3-2 win they didn't really deserve. City were the better side and Mark Robins and Iwan Roberts found the target, but Kalac's mistakes undid all the good work from Mark McGhee's team.

SATURDAY 9TH NOVEMBER 1957

Matt Gillies' team were finding it tough in the top flight after storming to the Second Division title the previous season and were on the receiving end of a 7-3 hammering at Burnley. Johnny Newman made his Foxes debut after joining from Birmingham City for £12,000 and could do little to stop the rampant Clarets. Leicester did lead twice in the first half thanks to John Doherty's goals and were eyeing a possible point when Derek Hogg netted after 79 minutes to make it 4-3. A late flurry of goals sank Leicester and left Burnley hat-trick heroes Jimmy McIlroy and Albert Cheesebrough to squabble over who should take home the match ball.

SATURDAY 9TH NOVEMBER 1929

Leicester City and Portsmouth clashed at Filbert Street – and there was a stunning reversal of fortunes. The previous season, City had romped to their record 10-0 win and the home fans must have harboured hopes of a repeat with Pompey having shipped 20 goals in their previous three games. Instead, the visitors upset the formbook and claimed a 5-0 win. City were without influential skipper Johnny Duncan and centre-half George Carr was back in the starting line-up despite not being fully fit. Pompey took advantage with Fred Forward netting twice.

SATURDAY 10TH NOVEMBER 1985

Goals from Ian Banks and Gary Lineker weren't enough to save Leicester City from defeat against Manchester United at Filbert Street. Gordon Milne's team were beaten 3-2 in the Division One clash.

WEDNESDAY 11TH NOVEMBER 1998

Weeks after Martin O'Neill's decision to stay at Leicester City rather than join Leeds United, the two sides met at Filbert Street in a cracking League Cup fourth round tie. Leeds took the lead through Harry Kewell's header that slipped through Leicester goalkeeper Kasey Keller's fingers, but there was late drama. Muzzy Izzet pulled City level with three minutes left in spectacular style. Leeds goalkeeper Nigel Martyn raced from his goal to head the ball clear and it fell to the City midfielder, who sent a sweetly-struck volley into the empty net. Izzet was then involved in City's winner in the dying moments. He was felled by Robert Molenaar for a penalty that Garry Parker stepped up to convert to send Leicester through.

SATURDAY 11TH NOVEMBER 1967

Frank Large made his Leicester City debut after joining from Northampton Town and he could not have had a tougher start. The Foxes were thrashed 6-0 at Manchester City in Division One.

SATURDAY 11TH NOVEMBER 1989

Paul Ramsey came off the bench and netted twice in a dramatic 4-3 win for David Pleat's Leicester City against Division Two pacesetters Leeds United at Filbert Street. Paul Moran and Gary McAllister got the other goals for the Foxes as they upset the formbook to win a seven-goal thriller with McAllister rolling home the winner to cap a sensational fightback. Kevin Campbell made his Leicester debut after arriving on loan from Arsenal. He became Pleat's second loan signing after Moran joined from Division One side Tottenham Hotspur.

SATURDAY 12TH NOVEMBER 1955

BBC Television's *Sportsview* programme put Leicester City under the spotlight for the first time and the presence of the cameras inspired the Foxes to a 6-1 demolition of Swansea Town in Division Two. Willie Gardiner was the hat-trick hero for the Foxes and the other goals came from Mal Griffiths, Johnny Morris and Arthur Rowley.

SATURDAY 13TH NOVEMBER 1965

George Best and Bobby Charlton were on the scoresheet for Manchester United in a 5-0 Division One thrashing of Leicester City at Filbert Street.

SATURDAY 13TH NOVEMBER 1982

Leicester City and Newcastle United fought out a thrilling 2-2 draw in Division Two at Filbert Street. Tommy English and Gary Lineker were on target for City and Kevin Keegan bagged both replies for the Magpies.

SATURDAY 14TH NOVEMBER 1970

Leicester City were given a helping hand by their opponents at Filbert Street. They were 3-1 winners over Swindon Town and two of the strikes were own goals. Ally Brown grabbed the other goal for the Foxes to make it four straight wins to keep his side on top of Division Two and on course for promotion.

SATURDAY 15TH NOVEMBER 1958

Leicester City striker Derek Hines netted four times in a 6-3 romp over Aston Villa at Filbert Street. Jimmy Walsh and Bernard Kelly got the other goals in the demolition.

WEDNESDAY 15TH NOVEMBER 1961

Leicester City's Uefa Cup second round second leg tie at Atletico Madrid attracted a crowd of 52,000. The sides were level at 1-1 from the first leg at Filbert Street and City boss Matt Gillies handed Graham Cross a place at the heart of the Foxes' defence on his 18th birthday. Cross acquitted himself well, along with goalkeeper Gordon Banks, who kept out a penalty. The City stopper was beaten by another penalty and Leicester bowed out to the eventual winners. Gillies expressed his displeasure at the officials and their decision to award two penalties following City's exit by 3-1 on aggregate.

SUNDAY 15TH NOVEMBER 1992

Julian Joachim was the two-goal hero for Brian Little's Leicester City in a 2-1 win at Sunderland in Division One that lifted them into the top six in the table.

SATURDAY 16TH NOVEMBER 1996

Leicester City's 3-1 win at Aston Villa gave further proof that Martin O'Neill's team were blossoming into a Premiership force. Steve Walsh was back in the side after a knee operation and Steve Claridge gave Leicester the perfect start with an eighth-minute goal. Villa drew level, but City led at the break after referee David Elleray awarded them a penalty just before the interval and Garry Parker rifled home. Leicester defended well in the second half and made sure of the points with seven minutes left when Muzzy Izzet latched on to Claridge's pass and rounded the goalkeeper to score.

SATURDAY 16TH NOVEMBER 1895

Leicester Fosse's biggest local rivals in their early years came from a few miles up the A6. Their games with Loughborough Town were hard fought and created plenty of interest. The games led to the first "football specials" on the railways and there were clashes between rival fans. Fosse proved they were Leicestershire's premier team with a 4-1 thumping at the Athletic Grounds in Loughborough that came a month after a 5-0 win. Town went ahead in the second meeting through an own goal from Harry Davy, but Fosse stormed back. Richard Davies found the target twice and the other goals came from Matt Bishop and James Lynes.

SATURDAY 16TH NOVEMBER 1957

Leicester City played their first game under the Filbert Street floodlights. The visitors were Preston North End for a Division One fixture and poor visibility meant the lights were switched on from the start of the game that kicked off at three o'clock. City were beaten 3-1 in the historic fixture with Tommy McDonald grabbing the goal for the Foxes.

SATURDAY 17TH NOVEMBER 1984

Ian Banks and Gary Lineker got the goals for Leicester City in a 2-0 win over Norwich City at Filbert Street in Division One to hand Gordon Milne's strugglers a boost.

SATURDAY 18TH NOVEMBER 1967

Len Glover made his Leicester City debut in a 2-2 draw against Arsenal at Filbert Street. Foxes boss Matt Gillies paid Charlton Athletic £80,000 – then a British record for a winger – to bring him to Filbert Street five years after his goal dumped Leicester out of the League Cup. Glover made a sparkling debut. He tormented Gunners full-back Peter Storey throughout and was a whisker away from scoring with a blistering shot that came back off the crossbar in front of the Kop. Frank Large, making his first home appearance for City, opened the scoring for the home side and Jackie Sinclair added a second from the penalty spot. But they had to settle for a point against an Arsenal side that included future Leicester players Frank McLintock, Jon Sammels and George Armstrong. The Gunners fought back to earn a share of the spoils.

SATURDAY 19TH NOVEMBER 1966

A crowd of 25,003 at Filbert Street saw goals from Leicester City strikers Mike Stringfellow and Derek Dougan clinch a 2-1 win over West Bromwich Albion and take the Foxes up to sixth in Division One.

SATURDAY 20TH NOVEMBER 1909

Fred Shinton bagged a hat-trick in just five minutes for Leicester Fosse in a 3-0 win over Oldham Athletic.

WEDNESDAY 21ST NOVEMBER 1962

Alan Smith was born in Birmingham.

SATURDAY 21ST NOVEMBER 1953

Derek Hines took just ten seconds to find the target for Leicester City in the Division Two clash against Lincoln City at Filbert Street. He finished the game with a five-goal haul in a 9-2 romp for the Foxes. The other goalscorers were Arthur Rowley (2), Johnny Morris and Mal Griffiths.

TUESDAY 22ND NOVEMBER 1994

Brian Little cited personal reasons for his decision to resign as Leicester City boss the day after Everton won the Merseyside derby to leave his Foxes side bottom of the Premier League.

WEDNESDAY 23RD NOVEMBER 1994

Leicester City went into the Premier League clash with Arsenal at Filbert Street in disarray. Boss Brian Little had walked out the previous day and City had lost their four previous games. Allan Evans was in charge and will be remembered for leaving with a 100 per cent record as Foxes boss after the team responded with a gutsy performance that secured a third Premiership win of the season. City were ahead after 16 minutes. Ian Ormondroyd took the plaudits from the majority of a 20,774 crowd, but the dubious goals panel later deemed it was an own goal by goalkeeper David Seaman. Ian Wright levelled the scores from the penalty spot, but David Lowe restored City's lead before the break and they held on in the second half to lift the gloom and raise hopes they could survive in the top flight.

SATURDAY 23RD NOVEMBER 1985

Leicester City were struggling at the bottom of Division One and Manchester United setting the pace at the top when the sides clashed at Filbert Street. Gordon Milne's team stunned the visitors with three goals in the opening 30 minutes that secured a famous victory. Gary McAllister put Leicester on their way with a sweetly-struck shot after just seven minutes and Alan Smith doubled the lead before thumping home the third from a tight angle to send the home fans wild.

SATURDAY 23RD NOVEMBER 1935

Leicester City went top of Division Two with victory at Filbert Street. Tony Carroll and Gene O'Callaghan got the goals in a 2-0 win over Plymouth Argyle.

TUESDAY 23RD NOVEMBER 1948

Frank Worthington was born in Halifax.

SATURDAY 24TH NOVEMBER 1979

Derek Strickland and Martin Henderson were on target for Leicester City in a 2-0 win over Wrexham at Filbert Street. The result stretched City's unbeaten run to six games and kept Jock Wallace's team fifth in Division Two.

IAN ORMONDROYD

FRIDAY 25TH NOVEMBER 1994

Brian Little was unveiled as Aston Villa's new boss. Leicester City fans were far from happy. Alan Evans, who had been in caretaker charge of City following Little's departure from Filbert Street, resigned. City fans were incensed because Little had said personal reasons had been behind his decision to quit Leicester just six months after taking them into the Premier League.

SATURDAY 25TH NOVEMBER 1989

A 1-0 win at Stoke City marked the start of a revival by David Pleat's Leicester City. He brought in loan strikers Paul Moran and Kevin Campbell from Tottenham Hotspur and Arsenal, respectively, and they played their part in a crucial victory that sparked a run of six wins in seven games. Both sides needed the points at the Victoria Ground. Stoke were bottom of the table and City just one point and one place above them. Gary Mills struck after 62 minutes to ease the relegation fears of Leicester's fans and move them away from their relegation rivals.

SATURDAY 25TH NOVEMBER 1961

Goalkeeper George Heyes was Leicester City's hero in a 2-1 win at Tottenham Hotspur in Division One. Heyes was beaten after just three minutes by John White's effort and City were level five minutes later through Ken Keyworth's strike from a Howard Riley cross. Hugh McIlmoyle went close to giving Leicester the lead with a header that crashed against the woodwork and then nodded down for Colin Appleton to lash home an unstoppable shot from 25 yards with 20 minutes left. The home side threw everything at Heyes in the last 20 minutes, but he kept them all out to secure maximum points for the Foxes.

SATURDAY 26TH NOVEMBER 1927

The first radio commentary from Filbert Street captured the drama as Leicester City beat Newcastle United 3-0 in Division One. Arthur Chandler grabbed two goals for City and Arthur Lochhead completed the scoring.

WEDNESDAY 27TH NOVEMBER 1895

Arthur Chandler was born in Paddington and he went on to become the record goalscorer in Leicester City's history.

WEDNESDAY 27TH NOVEMBER 1991

Brian Little's Leicester City beat Premier League Everton in the third round of the Zenith Data Systems Cup at Filbert Street. David Oldfield put City ahead with a thunderbolt and Steve Thompson doubled the lead before Peter Beardsley danced through to halve the arrears for the Toffeemen. City held on to the lead.

SATURDAY 27TH NOVEMBER 1976

Leicester City stayed sixth in Division One following a 2-2 draw at Leeds United. Frank Worthington and Steve Earle got the goals for City at Elland Road.

SATURDAY 27TH NOVEMBER 1993

Iwan Roberts made a stunning debut for Leicester City after joining from Huddersfield Town for a fee of £300,000. He netted twice in a dramatic 2-2 draw against Wolverhampton Wanderers at Filbert Street and was a whisker away from completing a hat-trick in a dramatic clash when he just failed to convert a cross.

SATURDAY 27TH NOVEMBER 1926

Foxes legend Arthur Chandler got all five goals for Leicester City in their 5-1 thrashing of Aston Villa at Filbert Street.

WEDNESDAY 27TH NOVEMBER 1996

Goals from Steve Claridge and Emile Heskey powered Leicester City to a 2-0 win over Manchester United in a League Cup fourth round tie at Filbert Street.

SATURDAY 28TH NOVEMBER 1981

Jock Wallace's Leicester City stormed to a 4-1 win over Cambridge United at Filbert Street that took them five places up the Division Two table to ninth. The goals came from Steve Lynex, Trevor Hebberd, Andy Peake and Gary Lineker.

SATURDAY 29TH NOVEMBER 1997

The wait for a win at Coventry City came to an end for Leicester City and their supporters. Their first win at the Sky Blues' home for 22 years came thanks to an opening goal from Graham Fenton and Matt Elliott's penalty.

WEDNESDAY 30TH NOVEMBER 1988

There's never a Russian linesman when you need one! Leicester City and Nottingham Forest battled out a goalless draw in the fourth round of the League Cup in front of a bumper crowd of 26,764 at Filbert Street. But, the scoreline should have been different according to Mike Newell. City's striker crashed a right-foot shot off the underside of the bar in the second half of a game played in a highly-charged atmosphere and is still convinced the ball crossed the line, two decades later. The linesman disagreed and the game ended scoreless. First Division Forest had to play the second half with only ten men after Stuart Pearce was dismissed for a reckless lunge on Paul Reid.

WEDNESDAY 30TH NOVEMBER 1983

A Leicester City legend marked his return to Filbert Street with a goal in a game that brought Foxes striker Gary Lineker face-to-face with his hero. Former City striker Frank Worthington was on target for Southampton, but it wasn't enough to prevent the Foxes running out 2-1 winners in the Division One clash. Alan Smith and Gary Lineker got the goals for Gordon Milne's team in front of 14,181 and that made it back-to-back wins for City as they put their disastrous start to the season behind them.

WEDNESDAY 30TH NOVEMBER 1966

Leicester City stayed fifth in Division One despite a 2-1 defeat at home to Manchester United. David Gibson grabbed City's goal and the replies for United came from George Best and Denis Law.

SATURDAY 30TH NOVEMBER 1968

Everton piled on the misery for Division One strugglers Leicester City at Goodison Park. Rodney Fern was on target for City in a crushing 7-1 defeat that made it eight games without a win for the Foxes. Joe Royle got a hat-trick for the Toffeemen.

LEICESTER CITY
On This Day

DECEMBER

SATURDAY 1ST DECEMBER 1990

Leicester City edged out Newcastle United in a nine-goal Division Two thriller at Filbert Street. David Kelly bagged a hat-trick for the Foxes and Mick Quinn hit a treble for the visitors. David Pleat's City included loan signings Mike Hooper and Terry Fenwick and they led 2-1 at the break through Fenwick and Kelly. David Oldfield and Kelly (penalty) made it 4-1 to the home side, but Newcastle hit back and reduced the deficit to a single goal with two strikes. Kelly appeared to have put the game beyond the visitors with the goal that completed his hat-trick after 86 minutes, but there was still time left for Quinn to bag his third and set up a nervy climax to the match.

TUESDAY 1ST DECEMBER 1964

Leicester City's record away win came at Coventry City on the day Foxes legend Ken Keyworth completed a switch to Highfield Road. He saw his former team storm to an 8-1 win in a League Cup fifth round tie over the Sky Blues, who were playing in the third tier of English football. Graham Cross had a spell in goal for Matt Gillies' team after Gordon Banks was injured and Coventry skipper George Curtis contributed an own goal as City went on the rampage. Full-back Richie Norman was on target twice for City, and they were collector's items. He scored just five times in 365 appearances.

WEDNESDAY 2ND DECEMBER 1998

Leicester City went through to the semi-finals of the League Cup with victory over Premier League rivals Blackburn Rovers at Filbert Street. Neil Lennon grabbed the only goal to set up a semi-final against Sunderland.

SATURDAY 2ND DECEMBER 2000

Leicester City went back up to third in the Premier League with a 3-1 win over Leeds United at Filbert Street that was secured by goals from Robbie Savage, Ade Akinbiyi and Gerry Taggart.

SATURDAY 3RD DECEMBER 1966

Teenager David Nish made a goalscoring debut in the 4-2 win over Stoke City at Filbert Street. Peter Rodrigues, Derek Dougan and John Sinclair got the other goals. Nish went on to play 272 games for the Foxes and score 31 goals.

SATURDAY 3RD DECEMBER 1994

Brian Little was barracked throughout the game as he returned to Filbert Street as manager of Aston Villa. Fans held banners declaring him 'Judas' and 'Liar'. Phil Gee's goal, that put Leicester City ahead, lightened the mood somewhat. Guy Whittingham grabbed a second-half equaliser. There can seldom have been such a hostile atmosphere at Filbert Street.

SATURDAY 4TH DECEMBER 1976

Leicester City were thumped 6-2 by Birmingham City at a frozen Filbert Street. The visitors coped better with the Arctic conditions and none more so than Kenny Burns, who grabbed a hat-trick for the Blues. Steve Kember and Frank Worthington got City's goals.

SATURDAY 5TH DECEMBER 1987

Leicester City and Middlesbrough battled out a goalless draw at Filbert Street in Division Two. The result made it four games without a win and left the Foxes 16th in the table. It proved to be Bryan Hamilton's last game in charge of the club.

SATURDAY 6TH DECEMBER 1980

Leicester City ended a run of four straight defeats in Division One with a 2-1 win at Birmingham City. Jim Melrose got both goals for City and Geoff Scott put through his own goal for the Blues' reply. Scott went on to join Birmingham City.

THURSDAY 7TH DECEMBER 1995

Mark McGhee was unveiled as Wolverhampton Wanderers' new manager after walking out of Leicester City just over 12 months after Brian Little quit the job. Leicester fans were furious and accused McGhee of betrayal. His response was to say: "I think everyone at Leicester knows what type of person I am." The response was emphatic, but unprintable.

SATURDAY 8TH DECEMBER 1984

Gordon Milne's team started their climb towards Division One safety with a 4-0 win at Sunderland. Leicester City stunned the home side with three goals in the first half. Alan Smith led the way with a double strike after 16 and 42 minutes and strike partner Gary Lineker added another. The scoring was completed by Steve Lynex after 71 minutes and City's strikeforce went on to hit top gear. Smith then proceeded to score in five successive games – and Lynex in four – to take the Foxes away from the drop zone, while Sunderland's slump continued and they ended up being relegated.

SATURDAY 9TH DECEMBER 1989

Kevin Campbell got his first goal for Leicester City after arriving on loan from Arsenal. He was on target in a 4-2 win at Blackburn Rovers. Gary McAllister got City's opening goal from the penalty spot and the others came from Simon Morgan and Tommy Wright.

SATURDAY 10TH DECEMBER 1977

Roger Davies, a hero in Derby County's First Division championship-winning season of 1974-75, made his Leicester City debut against the Rams in a 1-1 draw at Filbert Street. Foxes boss Frank McLintock splashed out a club record £250,000 to bring Davies to the club from Belgian football in a bid to boost his side's survival hopes in Division One.

FRIDAY 10TH DECEMBER 1999

Darren Eadie became Leicester City's record signing when he joined from Norwich City for a fee of £3m.

FRIDAY 11TH DECEMBER 1987

Bryan Hamilton was sacked as Leicester City manager with the Foxes 16th in Division Two.

SATURDAY 12TH DECEMBER 1987

Peter Morris took charge of the Leicester City team that was beaten 2-0 at Oldham Athletic in the first game following Bryan Hamilton's departure. Tommy Wright, who went on to become a fans' favourite at Filbert Street, got one of the goals for the Latics in the Division Two clash.

DARREN EADIE

SATURDAY 13TH DECEMBER 1947

Goalkeeper Joe Calvert became Leicester City's oldest-ever player when he went between the posts at Southampton at the age of 40 years and 313 days. City were beaten 3-1.

WEDNESDAY 14TH DECEMBER 1994

Mark McGhee became Leicester City's new manager after quitting Reading.

WEDNESDAY 14TH DECEMBER 1988

Leicester City crashed out of the League Cup after defeat at East Midlands rivals Nottingham Forest in their fourth round replay. The sides had drawn 0-0 at Filbert Street and Forest went ahead in the replay through Gary Crosby. City levelled when Paul Groves headed home a Mike Newell cross. Forest roared back and Lee Chapman stabbed home the winner after a goalmouth scramble.

WEDNESDAY 15TH DECEMBER 1999

Leicester City had never won a penalty shoot-out until the visit of Leeds United for a League Cup fourth round tie at Filbert Street. Their three previous shoot-outs had all ended in defeat, but that all changed after 120 minutes of stalemate. City went first and Icelandic international Arnar Gunnlaugsson kept his cool to slot home the opener. Matt Elliott and Andrew Impey were also successful to keep Leicester ahead at 3-2 and Leeds defender Gary Kelly then blazed over the bar to put the home side in charge. Theo Zagorakis then shot over, but Leeds midfielder Ian Bowyer also cracked under the pressure. He smacked his shot against the crossbar and Muzzy Izzet netted Leicester's next spot kick to send his team through 4-2.

SATURDAY 15TH DECEMBER 1951

A third successive win in December against promotion rivals Cardiff City lifted Norman Bullock's Leicester City up to sixth place in Division Two. Arthur Rowley gave the Foxes the perfect start with a 10th-minute opener and Derek Hines gave the home side some breathing space by doubling the lead just before the hour mark. Fred Worthington completed the scoring with a third goal.

TUESDAY 16TH DECEMBER 1969

Simon Grayson was born in Ripon, Yorkshire. He went on to become the first Leicester City captain to lift a trophy at Wembley.

SATURDAY 16TH DECEMBER 1961

Goals from Albert Cheesebrough and Jimmy Walsh secured a 2-0 win over Manchester City at Filbert Street in Division One.

SUNDAY 17TH DECEMBER 1995

A huge day in Leicester City's history: Martin O'Neill quit as Norwich City manager on the morning of the game with the Canaries at Filbert Street. Mike Walker was at the match working as a television pundit and was expected to become City's next manager after Mark McGhee's departure. Leicester hit back from 2-0 down to win 3-2 and Walker didn't get the job. O'Neill did.

SATURDAY 17TH DECEMBER 1994

Mark McGhee's first game in charge of Leicester City ended in a goalless draw against Premier League table-toppers Blackburn Rovers at Filbert Street. It was the Foxes' first clean sheet of the season and Rovers went on to win the title.

SATURDAY 18TH DECEMBER 1999

Darren Eadie made his Leicester City debut eight days after becoming the club's record £3m signing and couldn't prevent a 1-0 defeat at Derby County in the Premier League.

SATURDAY 18TH DECEMBER 1954

Andy Graver marked his Leicester City debut with a goal in a 3-1 defeat at Chelsea in Division One. Graver became City's record signing when he joined from Lincoln City for a fee of £27,600. The game is also remembered for a bizarre 'shared' own goal. Stan Milburn and Jack Froggatt simultaneously kicked the ball past Foxes keeper Johnny Anderson.

SUNDAY 19TH DECEMBER 1993

Leicester City avoided defeat at Peterborough United thanks to a last-gasp own goal, after Tony Adcock's opener had put the Posh on course for a league double, after victory at Filbert Street earlier in the season.

SATURDAY 20TH DECEMBER 1974

Keith Weller refused to come out for the second half of the game against Ipswich Town at Filbert Street. Weller had a transfer request turned down a few days before the game and got his wish after the game along with a fine of two weeks' wages.

SATURDAY 21ST DECEMBER 1963

Frank McLintock got the only goal for Leicester City in a 1-0 win at Arsenal in Division One.

SATURDAY 22ND DECEMBER 1973

Frank Worthington's late goal settled the local derby against Coventry City at Filbert Street, just three days before Christmas. The win also took Jimmy Bloomfield's team up to fifth place in Division One, but it was the Sky Blues who started the better as they led through a ninth-minute goal. City were level at the break thanks to Len Glover, who blasted home an unstoppable shot from the edge of the penalty area just moments before half-time. Leicester, with new signing Steve Earle in the thick of the action, stepped up a gear after the break. But, they had to wait until two minutes before the end of the match for the decisive goal. Worthington rose to head home Glover's cross to break Coventry's hearts.

SATURDAY 22ND DECEMBER 1934

Leicester City's home game against Portsmouth kicked off with only one official on duty. Referee FW Wort didn't arrive until half-time and one of the linesmen didn't arrive until the third minute. That left AW Smith to take charge and the sides shared four goals in a hectic opening seven minutes. City went on to win 6-3 with Arthur Chandler netting twice. The haul was rounded up by Tommy Mills, Arthur Maw, Danny Liddle and an own goal.

SATURDAY 23RD DECEMBER 1995

Martin O'Neill's first game as Leicester City manager ended in a 2-2 draw at Grimsby Town. The goals came from Iwan Roberts and Steve Walsh.

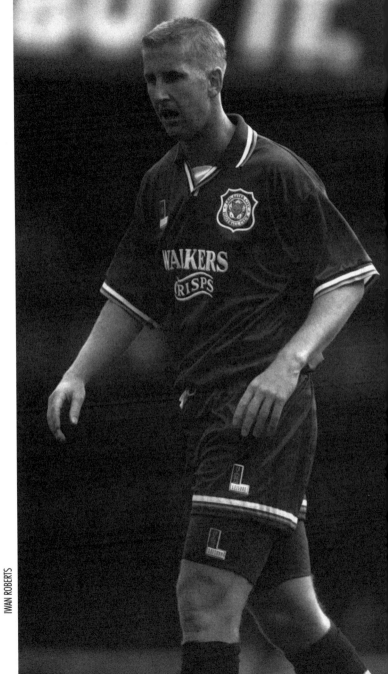

SATURDAY 24TH DECEMBER 1932

Leicester City were edged out 4-3 at West Bromwich Albion. City's marksmen in the seven-goal thriller in Division One were Arthur Lochhead, John Campbell and Sep Smith.

THURSDAY 25TH DECEMBER 1924

John Duncan bagged six goals in the 7-0 thrashing of Port Vale at Filbert Street. Arthur Chandler had opened the scoring for the Foxes in the Division Two clash in front of a crowd of 22,000. The result kept City fourth in the table.

FRIDAY 25TH DECEMBER 1953

Leicester City stayed top of the Division Two table with a 4-1 thumping of Rotherham United at Filbert Street. Arthur Rowley was the goal hero with a hat-trick and Derek Hines bagged the other for the Foxes in front of a bumper crowd of 30,902.

SATURDAY 25TH DECEMBER 1926

Arthur Chandler made it a happy Christmas for Leicester City fans with a five-goal haul in his team's 5-0 thrashing of West Bromwich Albion at Filbert Street. The result lifted the Foxes up to fifth in Division One.

MONDAY 26TH DECEMBER 1932

Andy Lochhead got his 100th goal for Leicester City in a 2-1 defeat at Portsmouth. It was his 267th game for City.

MONDAY 27TH DECEMBER 1993

For thousands of Leicester City fans, Ian Ormondroyd saved Christmas. He sent a last-gasp header looping into Watford's net to snatch a dramatic 4-4 draw at Filbert Street. The other scorers for Brian Little's team were David Oldfield (2) and a Steve Thompson penalty.

MONDAY 28TH DECEMBER 1959

Albert Cheesebrough gave Leicester City the lead after just 13 seconds of the game at Preston North End. City had to settle for a point after a 1-1 draw. The result made it five games unbeaten for City in Division One.

SATURDAY 29TH DECEMBER 1979

Two goals in the last seven minutes ensured Leicester City ended the decade with a win. Jock Wallace's promotion hopefuls took on Queens Park Rangers at Filbert Street and the visitors went on the defensive after the dismissal of future City defender Bob Hazell. Leicester dominated, hitting the woodwork twice, but couldn't find a way through until Dennis Rofe broke the deadlock. He carried the ball out of defence, the visitors backed off and Rofe belted home a stunning shot from 30 yards. With two minutes left, Martin Henderson doubled the lead with a header from close range.

SATURDAY 29TH DECEMBER 1973

Leicester City's 2-0 win at Arsenal completed a rare double over the Gunners and lifted Jimmy Bloomfield's team up to fifth in Division One. City's two-goal hero at Highbury was Frank Worthington. Worthington ensured he found the target for the fifth successive game with a 12th-minute opener to boost his hopes of an England call-up and he set up the second after 17 minutes. He lashed a fierce effort goalwards that Steve Earle diverted into the net with his head. Both players claimed the goal and it was Earle who eventually got the credit for what was his 100th goal in the Football League.

SATURDAY 29TH DECEMBER 1934

Arthur Chandler scored in a 3-1 defeat at Wolverhampton Wanderers and that made him Leicester City's oldest-ever goalscorer at the age of 39 years and 32 days. It was the last goal of a record-breaking City career that brought 273 goals in 419 appearances.

FRIDAY 30TH DECEMBER 1938

Gordon Banks was born in Sheffield and went on to become a goalkeeping legend for both Leicester City and England.

SATURDAY 31ST DECEMBER 1960

Leicester City hammered Everton 4-1 at Filbert Street in Division One. Ken Leek netted twice for the Foxes while the other strikes came from Howard Riley and Jimmy Walsh.